Conversations with Rudolfo Anaya

Literary Conversations Series

Peggy Whitman Prenshaw
General Editor

Photo credit: ©Michael Mouchette, courtesy of University of New Mexico Press
Literary Conversations Series

Conversations
with Rudolfo Anaya

Edited by
Bruce Dick and Silvio Sirias

University Press of Mississippi
Jackson

Copyright © 1998 by University Press of Mississippi
Manufactured in the United States of America

01   00   99   98   4   3   2   1

The paper in this book meets the guidelines for permanence and durability of the Committee on Production Guidelines for Book Longevity of the Council on Library Resources.

Library of Congress Cataloging-in-Publication Data

Anaya, Rudolfo A.
    Conversations with Rudolfo Anaya / edited by Bruce Dick and Silvio
Sirias.
        p.   cm. — (Literary conversations series)
    Includes index.
    ISBN 1-57806-077-X (alk. paper). — ISBN 1-57806-078-8 (pbk. :
alk. paper)
    1. Anaya, Rudolfo A.—Interviews.   2. Novelists, American—20th
century—Interviews.   3. Mexican American authors—Interviews.
4. Mexican Americans—Intellectual life.   5. Mexican Americans in
literature.   I. Dick, Bruce, 1953–   .   II. Sirias, Silvio.
III. Title.   IV. Series.
PS3551.N27Z464   1998
813'.54—dc21
    [B]   98-24028
                                                                CIP

British Library Cataloging-in-Publication Data available

Books by Rudolfo Anaya

Bless Me, Ultima. Berkeley: Quinto Sol Publications, 1972.
Heart of Aztlan. Berkeley: Editorial Justa Publications, 1976.
Tortuga. Berkeley: Editorial Justa Publications, 1979.
The Silence of the Llano. Berkeley: Quinto Sol/Tonatiuh Publications, 1982.
The Adventures of Juan Chicaspatas. Houston: Arte Público Press, 1985.
A Chicano in China. Albuquerque: University of New Mexico Press, 1986.
The Farolitos of Christmas. Santa Fe: New Mexico Magazine, 1987.
Lord of the Dawn: The Legend of Quetzalcoatl. Albuquerque: University of New Mexico Press, 1987.
Alburquerque. Albuquerque: University of New Mexico Press, 1992.
Zia Summer. New York: Warner Books, 1995.
Rudolfo Anaya Reader. New York: Warner Books, 1995.
Jalamanta. New York: Warner Books, 1996.
Rio Grande Fall. New York: Warner Books, 1996.
Maya's Children. New York: Hyperion, 1997.

Contents

Introduction

Rudolfo Anaya is one of the leading Chicano writers today. Since the release of *Bless Me, Ultima,* his groundbreaking first novel, in 1972, Anaya has published seven additional novels, a collection of short stories, a travel journal, an epic poem, and several plays. He also has edited or co-edited three fiction anthologies. His work has received widespread praise throughout the Latino literary community, earning him such laudatory epithets as "Godfather and guru of Chicano literature," "one of the founding fathers of Chicano literature," "the most acclaimed and universal Chicano writer," and "our poet of the llano and the barrio." Despite these accolades, the American reading public has yet to fully discover Anaya's talent, even after his twenty-five years as a published writer. The problem resides primarily in the publishing industry, which historically has neglected or rejected Latino/Latina writers. For example, Anaya circulated *Bless Me, Ultima* for several years before Quinto Sol, an independent press in Berkeley, California, finally published it. It was a full twenty-two years later before Warner Books, a major American publisher, distributed a mass market edition. Several of Anaya's other books have met similar fates.

As *Conversations with Rudolfo Anaya* illustrates, Anaya has finally achieved the critical recognition he deserves. This collection of fifteen interviews, spanning from 1976 to the present, reveals a writer who has remained acutely aware of the power of his words. Even though he is careful, even guarded, in many of his responses, Anaya is always eloquent. Throughout these interviews a surprising consistency in his views emerges on a wide range of subjects. While he cautions that all writers change over the years and should thus be allowed to modify their viewpoints, Anaya's vision and his awareness of the role of Chicano literature within American letters remains both consistent and optimistic from the first interview to the last. This optimism is admirable considering the difficulties most ethnic writers have experienced breaking into the American mainstream during the previous three decades.

Because of the ongoing success of *Bless Me, Ultima,* many of the interviews included here focus on this book. With unvarying patience, Anaya

answers the seemingly endless questions about his first published novel.
Rarely is he bothered that his other work is given secondary status. In fact,
when asked by Ray González whether *Bless Me, Ultima* has been a gift or a
hindrance to his career, Anaya responds: "Every author should be so lucky
to have a first novel stay around [for] 20 years." In several interviews he
acknowledges that his formative years constitute much of the fodder for his
first three novels, especially *Bless Me, Ultima.* The rural New Mexico setting
strongly resembles Santa Rosa, where Anaya spent most of his childhood.
The plot traces the spiritual journey of a young boy torn between Catholicism
and mysticism, a struggle which Anaya admits experiencing during his own
youth. Despite the similarities, Anaya downplays the idea that these narra-
tives accurately depict his life. He states in an early interview with David
Johnson and David Apodoca that even though his "writing is biographical"
he is "not concerned about it being true to reality."

New Mexico is the imaginative terrain from which most of his writing
originates, Anaya suggests, because he is inextricably tied to this land. In a
conversation with Juan Bruce-Novoa in 1978, he states that he has "no desire
to leave New Mexico." He emphasizes this same determination in his 1997
interview with Bruce Dick and Silvio Sirias: "New Mexico is home, stability,
and history. It has the feel of my ancestors. Their spirits are here. They speak
to me. If all this is happening and I live in a spiritual place, why would I
leave?" Visualizing the topography of the American southwest is central to
understanding Anaya's writing. He readily acknowledges that his artistic
imagination is indebted to the mystical powers of his birthplace and to his
belief in the spiritual permanence of humans to the regions they once inhab-
ited. The earth itself, for Anaya, reflects both the divine and the supernatural.
"The gods come from the sea and the trees and the mountains and the caves
and the forest, and people responding to those landscapes are responding to
those gods," he tells Feroza Jussawalla in an interview published in 1992.
"By responding to the gods you're responding to the landscapes. Different
landscapes give rise to a different form of gods and demons."

In these interviews Anaya often describes how mythology is linked to the
New Mexican landscape. In his writing he has created or recreated myths that
represent his philosophical preoccupations, including the Golden Carp in
Bless Me, Ultima; The Legend of La Llorona; and the Lords and Ladies of
Light in *Jalamanta* and the Sonny Baca mystery series. His adept use of
myth explores the fundamental human concerns of life and death, the supernatural, and fear of the unknown. Anaya maintains that we often fail to estab-

lish meaningful relationships because we have failed to realize the importance of myths. His resolute belief that myths can help redeem us leads to his
deep interest in encoding archetypes into his writing. Like Carl Jung, for
whom he often expresses admiration, Anaya subscribes to a belief in the
collective unconscious. His inclusion of archetypal symbols in his work emphasizes the continuities of human existence from past to present and mini-
mizes historical differences among people. Anaya states in a 1986 interview
with John Crawford that his novels constitute an "archetypal journey." He
explains to González-T. a year earlier that the archetype is "a primal symbol.
. . . It is in the creation of art that we take those primal symbols or those
archetypal symbols and infuse them into art . . . what they become is a
reflection that then speaks back to us because so many of those come from
the subconscious."

A cornerstone of Anaya's writings and a leitmotif that reappears in the
interviews is his preoccupation with spiritual matters. Culture and one's roots
are, for Anaya, inextricably linked to spiritual belief. In the interview with
González-T., he argues that his focus on spirituality began when a crisis of
faith distanced him from Catholicism: "I didn't think the church was providing everything that I needed. I also think that in many respects the church
has been an institution that, to be quite blunt, has been repressive in the lives
of people." In his interview with Dick and Sirias, Anaya suggests that his
personal theology is most fully illustrated in his novella, *Jalamanta.* In this
work Anaya puts his spiritual "questions and answers all together" in fictional form.

In the interviews Anaya also talks eloquently about his craft. He treasures
his membership in the writing profession and feels blessed at being able to
work at what he loves best. Specific questions focusing on Anaya's daily
writing habits, his relationship with editors, and his audience are best explored in the interview with Laura Chavkin, conducted in 1995. He speaks
openly about his art in other interviews, explaining that he rarely conducts
research when writing novels. While acknowledging that what applies to him
does not apply to all fiction writers, he explains to Johnson and Apodaca: "I
don't like research. I think research is harmful to the writer. . . . In research
you wind up telling somebody else's idea." He tells Dick and Sirias: "I think
the instinct of the writer is always to jump into the work, especially if it has
a kick to it, if it has something to say." However, Anaya does spend a significant amount of time rewriting his work. This revision process certainly
applies to *Bless Me, Ultima,* which he rewrote seven times. He does not

revise as painstakingly today as in the beginning of his career because "one gets better at what one does over the course of a lifetime."

Like most writers, Anaya's feeling towards critics is ambivalent. He acknowledges the importance of examining literary works closely, and in several interviews urges critics to study works by Chicano writers. He recognizes that academic study of Chicano literature will hasten its acceptance within American letters. Regarding his own work, however, Anaya reiterates that he is not concerned with what critics say or with how they respond to his work. Moreover, in various interviews, he argues that young authors should never write to please critics because such writing stifles creativity. In the interview with Bruce–Novoa conducted during the waning years of the Chicano Movement, Anaya states that he was at odds with numerous Chicano critics who believed that all works should contain a strong, overt political message: "Many Chicano critics find themselves in the Marxist-Leninist camp, where they deride and verbally abuse writers who will not cater to their personal and social needs. What such critics forget is that every man's or woman's creative, imaginative endeavor is an act of rebellion."

As these conversations demonstrate, Anaya has experienced a significant change in the arena of politics. In the earlier interviews he seems less certain about his political voice. He expresses his displeasure to Johnson and Apodaca over what he perceives as unfair pressure put on Chicano writers to be political. In a 1976 interview with Ishmael Reed, he shows similar concerns. By the 1980s, however, Anaya emerges as a self-assured spokesperson for Chicano causes. He tells John Crawford in 1986 that "there is even more need now for what we call a political stance, in our poetry and our novels." The following year, in an interview with Rubén Martínez, Anaya argues that literature must be subversive, that it must fight, in the age of multiculturalism, against the hegemony that one culture may attempt to exercise over another. Eight years later he tells Laura Chavkin that writers have an obligation to be political in order to take a strong stance against "hate, prejudice, and bigotry."

Anaya is most persuasive when he defines ethnicity and articulates the role he and others played in the Chicano Movement. "The word 'Chicano' to me," he tells Paul Vassallo in 1988, "means a particular group under [the] Hispanic umbrella. More specifically, it means . . . those of us who believed in the Chicano movement[,] worked in it[,] and . . . made a commitment to the image which the word 'Chicano' seems to define. And that image has to do with . . . understanding ourselves not only as Hispanics—as people of

Spanish and Mexican origins—but as people who also share in the Native American origin and the Native American heritage." According to Anaya the Chicano Movement not only prevented total assimilation into the cultural mainstream but attacked, and subsequently changed, the peripheral position Chicanos occupied in American society.

Understandably Anaya has been an important advocate for integrating multiculturalism in the classroom. An educator for over thirty-years, he has adamantly defended the perspectives of minorities and non-Western cultures, far before such a position became politically fashionable. Anaya has consistently waged a war against marginalizing minorities, arguing that the dominant culture has stripped them of any claim to centrality and power. For Anaya this exclusion extends deep into the literary marketplace. He repeatedly speaks of the difficulty Chicano writers have had publishing their work. In his 1987 interview with Martínez, he argues that the giants of the publishing industry have steadfastly rejected works by Mexican-American writers: "It is fair to say that the major publishers in this country are now closed to Chicanos. We simply are not accepted there." At the same time Anaya is adamant that the mainstream publishers should not define minority writers. He tells Bruce-Novoa as early as 1979, "We have to come out of our own experience, our own tradition, culture, roots, our own sense of language, of story, and deal with that and to hell with the white model."

As a founding father of Chicano literature, Anaya has a clear understanding of the Mexican-American literary voice. In his interview with Chavkin, he details the features that unite Chicano writers: "the language, the history, the folklore, the mythical beliefs underlying the multicultural roots that are our heritage, the relationship that we have to Anglo-America, the encounter with Anglo-America that occurred in the mid-nineteenth century, the continuing sense of tension between the two communities." Since *Ultima,* Anaya has fought against marginalizing non-Anglo fiction. Through his efforts, Chicano literature has not only escaped the inhibiting intellectual structures of the literary mainstream but kept its unique vision intact.

The interviews gathered here allow a glimpse into Anaya's imagination and art. They also provide a new understanding of his formative role in the shaping of American culture and thought. Anaya's persistence and talent have helped open the doors for a younger generation of Latino and Latina writers, including Sandra Cisneros, Ana Castillo, Julia Alvarez, Oscar Hijuelos, Cristina García, Denise Chávez, Benjamín Alire Sáenz, Virgil Suárez, Roberto Fernández, and many others. Increasingly greater critical attention is being given to Anaya's work. This collection should not only open doors for additional scholarship but help garner support for other Latino and Latina writers Anaya so gallantly represents.

These interviews have been reprinted uncut as they originally appeared. Typographical errors and clear errors of fact have been corrected. Because each interview originated and was executed as an independent project, there is unavoidable repetition with some questions. Nevertheless the variations of Anaya's answers are always revealing.

Several people who assisted in the completion of this book should be acknowledged. We would like to thank Seetha A-Srinivasan of the University Press of Mississippi for believing in this project. Mark Vogel, Diana Moody, Bill Pillow, Laura Flowers, and Chantal Dennis Morales of Appalachian State University offered invaluable help along the way. Michael Sirias assisted at various stages of the process. Thanks too to Wendy Sirias who applied her library talents during the initial stages and for coming to our aid again near the end, and to Gabriella Motta-Passajou for her patience and support. Many of the interviewers and scholars involved with Rudolfo Anaya's work contributed advice: Ray González, Rubén Sosa Villegas, Rubén Martínez, María Teresa Márquez, Ishmael Reed, and Virgil Suárez among them. César González-T. and Phyllis Morgan supplied valuable information on Anaya's biography and canon. Special thanks to the Appalachian State University Office of the Dean of the College of Arts and Sciences, and to the ASU Appalachian Humanities Program. Finally we are indebted to Rudolfo Anaya, whose support over the last year made the completion of this volume possible.

Chronology

1937   Born 30 October, to Rafaelita and Martín Anaya in Pastura, New Mexico; family moves to Santa Rosa, New Mexico, soon after Anaya's birth; grows up in Santa Rosa with three older brothers and six sisters.

1952   Family moves to Albuquerque, New Mexico; enters ninth grade at Washington Junior High School.

1956   Graduates from Albuquerque High School; attends Browning Business School (1956–1958).

1963   Receives Bachelor of Arts degree in English from the University of New Mexico; teaches English in Albuquerque public schools (1963–1968).

1966   Marries Patricia Lawless.

1968   Receives Master of Arts degree in English from the University of New Mexico.

1972   Serves as Director of Counseling at the University of Albuquerque until 1974; *Bless Me, Ultima,* a novel, is published; receives Premio Quinto Sol National Chicano Literature Award for *Bless Me, Ultima;* receives Master of Arts in Guidance and Counseling from the University of New Mexico.

1974   Begins teaching creative writing at the University of New Mexico; board member of CCLM and founder of the Rio Grande Writers Association.

1976   *Heart of Aztlan,* a novel, is published; co-edits *Voices from the Río Grande.*

1979   *Tortuga,* a novel, is published; *The Season of La Llorona,* a play, is first performed in Albuquerque; *Bilingualism: Premise for Tomorrow,* a screenplay, appears.

1980   Reads at the White House; receives a National Endowment for the Arts Fellowship; receives New Mexico Governor's Award; translates

Cuentos: Tales from the Hispanic Southwest (the book is a bilingual edition); receives Before Columbus Foundation's American Book Award for *Tortuga.*

1981   Co-edits *Ceremony of Brotherhood,* an anthology; honorary Doctor of Humane Letters from the University of Albuquerque.

1982   *The Silence of the Llano,* a collection of short stories, is published; receives a three year W. K. Kellogg Foundation National Fellowship.

1983   Co-edits *Chicanos: A Short Story Anthology;* begins Kellogg Foundation Fellowship (1983–1986).

1984   *The Legend of La Llorona,* a novella, is published; receives Doctor of Humane Letters, Marycrest College, Davenport, Iowa.

1985   *The Adventures of Juan Chicaspatas,* an epic poem, is published; attends Frankfurt Book Fair.

1986   *A Chicano in China,* a travel journal, is published; lectures in Israel, Paris, and Bordeaux, France.

1987   *Lord of the Dawn: The Legend of Quetzalcoatl,* a novel, is published; *The Farolitos of Christmas,* a short story, is published and is first performed as a play by La Compania; edits *Voces: An Anthology of Nuevo Mexicano Writers; Who Killed Don José,* a play, is produced.

1989   Edits *Tierra: Contemporary Short Fiction of New Mexico,* an anthology; co-edits *Aztlan: Essays on the Chicano Homeland;* delivers 34th Annual Research Lecture at University of New Mexico; travels in Egypt.

1990   Receives University of New Mexico Regents' Meritorious Service Award; receives PEN Center USA West Freedom to Write Award.

1992   *Alburquerque,* a novel, is published; world premier of *Matachines,* a play; receives Honorary Doctor of Humane Letters, University of New England.

1993   Receives PEN Center USA West Award for *Alburquerque;* retires from teaching.

1994   *Bless Me, Ultima* is reissued by Warner Books; Erma S. Fergusson Award from University of New Mexico Alumni Association; receives Honorary Doctor of Humane Letters, California Lutheran University.

1995   *Zia Summer,* a novel, is published; *The Anaya Reader* is published;

The Farolitos of Christmas, a children's book, is published by Hyperion.

1996   *Rio Grande Fall,* a novel, is published; *Jalamanta,* a novel, is published.

1997   *Maya's Children,* a children's book, is published; *Descansos/Tres Voces* published with Estevan Arellano and Denise Chávez; receives Honorary Doctor of Humane Letters, University of New Hampshire.

1998   Receives "Spirit of the West" Literary Achievement Award from Mountain and Plains Booksellers Association.

Conversations with Rudolfo Anaya

An Interview with Rudolfo Anaya

Ishmael Reed / 1976

From *The San Francisco Review of Books,* 4.2(1978):9–12, 34. Reprinted by permission of Ishmael Reed.

Rudolfo A. Anaya is a leading Chicano novelist. His first novel, *Bless Me, Ultima,* is a startling work about Afro-Indian religion and Southwest violence. It was published by Tonatiuh International, Inc., in Berkeley, California. It has sold 80,000 copies without a review in the major media. His second novel, *Heart of Aztlan,* was published by Editorial Justa, Inc.

The West is still in many ways New Spain, and some of the old feuds between Hispanic people and the Anglo-Saxon invaders surface from time to time. A few weeks before I interviewed Rudolfo Anaya, a confrontation between the competing groups had occurred over Mexican-Spanish land titles.

I interviewed Mr. Anaya on July 1, 1976, after an elegant breakfast of melons and french toast. From the porch of his custom-designed adobe house, I could view one of those warm, speckless, Southwest blue skies.

Reed: Do you prefer the term Chicano or Latino? Or Hispanic?

Anaya: Well, in New Mexico the two terms that are most widely used are Hispano and Chicano. I prefer Chicano.

IR: Hispano and Chicano. Okay, is there a friction between Anglos—by that I mean White, Whites of European descent—and Chicanos in New Mexico?

RA: What you have here in the Southwest are settled populations that were here a very, very long time. You have the Native American, you have the Pueblos, and then later you have the Spaniard, the Mexican. The friction occurs because the people who moved here from the East had a different philosophy, a different world view—a view that was very, very aggressive. And it meant manipulating land and resources in a different way. So *that* conflict began to exist and it still does. The land issue is at the very core of these problems, throughout, say, northern New Mexico and many other places in the Southwest, where communal lands, land grants, that people had were disrupted.

1

IR: By the coming of Anglo-Americans?

RA: Right. You know, that the people that were here, the Indian and the Mexican settlers, lost their land and almost lost their cultures. So that kind of conflict still exists. It erupts every once in awhile. I was telling you last night about this town across the mountain here in the Manzano mountains, Chilili. Just a few weeks ago, you know, the issue erupted. It's communal land. That's the issue. The fact is that we have very limited resources. This is semi-arid land, you know, you can do grazing and you can do minerals, and that's about it. There's a lot of competition for the *good* land, and it happened that the land got taken over through devious, nefarious ways. Since the 1840s when the easterners came in we have had that kind of a conflict going. The other conflict is one of wealth or money. Who has the money? Who is able to afford better housing, better education, better medical care? Who controls the power?

IR: You say the Whites are at the top? I mean, in terms of owning land and wealth?

RA: Yes, that's one of the things that makes for some hostile feelings in the environment. It seems to me when the people look around, like the Native American or the Chicano, and asks how come my kids aren't going to college? How come I'm the guy that's hauling the city's garbage? How come I'm the one that's on seasonable labor, you know, deal more with unemployment? You look around and you see who has better social benefits. And when your kids aren't getting an equal share then it's time to change things. And, the thing about it is, I think, that we're not doing enough about that. I think everyone should be doing a lot more because people begin to equate superior and inferior stances with this kind of situation that exists, and that leads to more cultural conflict.

IR: Who are the people who are the officials and who are armed? Is that mostly White? Or do you have Native Americans and . . .

RA: Everyone is armed—

IR: Do these conflicts often blow up into violence? You mentioned this incident that took place a few weeks ago where the Chicano people had their own sheriff. They had a rival sheriff to the county sheriff—

RA: Yeah. Ever since Tijerina and the courthouse raid of Tierra Amarilla you have . . .

IR: What is that? Would you go into that?

RA: Well, what's it been now, uh, ten years? You had a group of people indigenous to a community, to a land grant, saying this is our land, it was granted to us. You know, it's a hundred or three or four hundred years old. We have the right to choose our mayor and our sheriff, to patrol this land. And so that's what Tijerina did in a sense. He said, you know, this is our right, if somebody disturbs the peace our sheriff should go take care of it. And that's all they were going to do that day is to make a citizen's arrest. It turned out to be a bigger blow-up, I think. That's essentially what happened here in Chilili. The men of the community, the people of the community, say let's elect our sheriff, let's elect our mayor. It's our community; it's just like any incorporated city in the United States. So they went and closed the road. You know, no more development!

IR: And, so they prevented people from coming in? They were arrested?

RA: They were arrested. The county sent out the sheriff and arrested ten, twenty people.

IR: In some parts of California once in a while we read about Native Americans and Chicanos who are really organized in terrorism because of these land disputes. Do you get that kind of thing down here?

RA: That's a sensitive area.

IR: Does this affect the culture movement here? Do these questions enter into poetry?

RA: That's what I was hoping you would ask, you know, is how does all this tie together? Art and Revolution. The interesting thing is how does what is happening politically, how does my political awareness figure into what I write. It's very important. I've been involved in the Chicano Movement since the '60s, primarily in education.

IR: To reform the liberal arts?

RA: No, the Movement is a social and political and aesthetic movement, you know, called the Chicano Movimiento. And at its core it has a kind of consciousness-raising effect. When the Mexican-American or the Chicano looks around him and raises all the questions you're raising, you know. Who controls the land, who controls the wealth, who controls the schools?

IR: And the question of identity comes in?

RA: Yeah. And what do I do about it? What is my image in this world? Then you begin to have the Chicano's aggressive movement towards the society that he found himself in, that was not reflecting, say, his image, so

I've worked with that in the realm of education since that's where I've been all, most of, my life, I guess. When I started writing, that was an issue that I had to face, how do I reflect what is happening out there? That's what I tried to do in *Heart of Aztlan*. There you have a group of people oppressed by the railroad, which is a big monster, run by forces that are not in the people's interest. They're out there somewhere controlling the destiny of these people. And I take a small group of people and show how they came into conflict with the railroad and what they did for themselves in terms of organizing, in terms of coming to grips with their situation. So, I do respond to the political situation. But, it's not only that, I think the Chicano literary movement, the by-product of the movement or a parallel force of that movement is interested not only in questions of the dialectic, but also is interested in questions of the aesthetic, and questions of form, of style, in literature.

IR: Tell me about the Rio Grande Writers, when did they begin?

RA: We met in April of '76, at the University of New Mexico. We invited people to come and read and we had workshops on different areas, Southwest literature, teaching poetry in high school, how to encourage high school teachers to get into the creative writing *and* how to start students early. And, we also formed at that time the Rio Grande Writers Association, an effort to get the writers of the state, small press people, editors, and teachers of creative writing, together to have some kind of force in dealing with school systems, and distributing our literature and making our writers known to the public. It's multicultural. In our association most writers in the state are getting along with each other, mixing with each other, understanding each other. We read each other and we understand. We did one small anthology, *Voices from the Rio Grande*. We want to do a Directory of Literary Sources, which would be valuable, again to teachers, librarians.

And then we're trying to keep our newsletter going. We publish four or five issues a year, trying to expose small literary magazines that never got exposure before.

IR: Would you say that you're a vital writing center in the country? What I'm driving at is, if I went around, and went to different regions, everybody would say that they're the best.

RA: No, we're not a Movement. And we're not a center in the sense that we all share one philosophy or are trying to develop.

IR: You couldn't say you do share one philosophy.

RA: I would really have to disagree with that vigorously. We don't set up

to espouse one way of writing, or even to be concerned with a Southwest
stance, at all. You look at our first anthology. There are people in there coming from all different directions. The fact that they live in the Southwest
might infuse part of this into their writing, or, part of the landscape, part of
what it means to be here. But, we don't go around looking for it. I say that
because I'm sure there would be members in our association who would also
resist that kind of molding.

IR: Could you give me about six prominent names whose work bears
watching?

RA: There's Leroy Quintana, who's working down in El Paso, but he's
from Albuquerque. I think he's got a lot of future and a lot of promise. Les
Romero, who works in Clovis for the Social Security Administration. He's
one of the best poets in this country right now, and he's a young guy. Orlando
Romero, Tony Márez, who teaches at Highlands University, has published
poems, but hasn't gotten a book together. He's really great, I think. There's
just so many, for example Gene Frumkin, whose work's well known in all
the older generation. David Johnson, who also teaches there. Other writers
are Leslie Silko, that we know, and Simon Ortiz, there are so many. We are
a vital center!

IR: At the conference in Austin, when they were having a women's panel,
you said that you'd come to hear women say something meaningful, something of depth, for a change. Were you teasing them?

RA: I was just teasing. Listen, I don't want to get into that. I get into a lot
of trouble when I speak about women. I've got old-world views.

IR: You teach a course in Chicano literature in which you talk about Chicano literature of the last ten years, though Chicano people have been here
for centuries. What about the previous literature? Where would you begin the
Chicano literature?

RA: Well, people have picked arbitrary dates. They've picked 1848, the
treaty, the signing of the Treaty of Guadalupe Hidalgo which ceded the
Southwest to the United States as a birth of the Chicano, this Mexican-
American who no longer has Mexico as a Motherland, but is now appearing,
a kind of No-Man's Land. His own homeland, you know, Aztlán, I deal a lot
with the literature of the last ten years that's been produced by the Movement.
There was a lot of writing in newspapers. But I'm more interested in the

Movement part. There's a kind of energy, you know, that once we grab hold of the material we'll do something with it.

IR: Well, when did you start writing?

RA: Oh. Back in the '60s. Late '50s, early '60s.

IR: How long did it take you to do *Bless Me, Ultima?*

RA: It took me a long time. It took me six or seven years, because I didn't know how to write, you know. I had to learn all the techniques.

IR: *Ultima* seems to be a multicultural book, I mean, I do get Christian elements in there, but I get other, uh, hints of lost traditions.

RA: Yeah. It's been very well-received, and it does deal, not only with a Judeo-Christian background that the character reflects because of his up-bringing, but it tries also to get beneath that into a mythology of his own past as it existed in this land.

IR: I guess that's the beginning of a national culture. Everybody goes through that. You know? Blacks did. We had to go back to our mythology, folklores, before we could really get started in the '60s. We're doing this California anthology and we found that in the nineteenth century that Lat-ino—Black—White seemed to write the same way. I mean European 'i's' type stanzas. Things like that. Then, all of a sudden something happens in the twentieth century, a breakaway, and people go back to their roots. Who are your early influences, writers? Or was it writing, or was it other art forms, or painting or sculpture?

RA: Mostly reading and, I guess, some painting, because I've painted. I used to paint a lot. Mostly reading and what you would call the classics, in a sense, and a lot of American literature. Modern American literature.

IR: Would you write for television? They say Chicano writers can't write. I read that in the *San Francisco Chronicle* magazine section. Someone, I think the Chicanos in Los Angeles, were asking why weren't any more scripts done by Chicano writers. They said they don't know of any Chicano writers. The actors agreed. The Chicano actors said, 'Yeah. We don't have any kind of literature yet.'

RA: No, I wouldn't. I don't think I'd like television. I might do a work or two. If it was a work that I had time with. I would not get into one of these series that would demand that you be there every day putting out junk.

IR: OK. Now, Native Americans object to the way they're depicted in the media. You know, the Asian-Americans don't like 'Charlie Chan.' We don't like Norman Lear. He said the Black writers can't write. Do you object to things like 'Chico and the Man'? All these things. Do you think they're stereotypes?

RA: Well, I don't watch that much tv. I think it's nonsense. The only things I watch are some documentaries or news, or things like that. It's the worst kind of drug that we have in America today. It blew its chance to educate people, to use bright writers, the works. I watched some of the Black shows, you know, that they have, once or twice, and I saw 'Chico and the Man' once, and then that's enough. You know what it's like, and you realize that travesty has been done. It's that thing I was telling you about awhile ago, you know? You universalize the experience so much that you wash it down, and after awhile it doesn't matter if it's Chicano or Black or White. It's all the same. It's all garbage.

IR: A lot of us collaborate with other artists. Do you find yourself, well, not collaborating, but being in contact with Chicano painters? Are there painters in your movement? Musicians?

RA: Yeah. I know a *lot* of the writers, especially the Chicano writers that are writing now. I know Tomás Rivera, Rolando Hinojosa. Right here in town we have the De Colores publication. José Armas, who writes and has produced a really nice publication. I know Ron Arias, who did a novel, and José Torres Metzger.

IR: You're constantly in contact with what's happening in California?

RA: In a way. I'm aware of it because I teach the literature. I'm not a socializer. I don't have to be with all the writers, but we respect each other.

IR: Give me five books that I could put down. Say, for the uninitiated, like myself, for the mass reader.

RA: You mean, like a novel?

IR: Novels or poetry.

RA: Tomás Rivera did one called . . . *y no se lo tragó la tierra,* translated means 'And the Earth Did Not Part.' That's a real classic.

IR: Who published that?

RA: Quinto Sol originally. So you can get it from them. They're now Tonatillo. Rolando Hinojosa did one called *Estampas del Valle.* He's one of the good writers in the Movement. Ron Arias did *The Road to Tamazunchale.* Very good. One of the best treatments of death that has been written in the last ten, twenty years and it happens to be by a Chicano writer. *Nambé Year One* by Orlando Romero. Also published by Tonatiuh. There are a couple of others that I might mention. *The Autobiography of a Brown Buffalo* by that California writer Acosta. I like those. I've used them, and the students like them.

IR: You're working on a third novel?

RA: I'm working on the third one. I've got a really good draft of it right now.

IR: You know, you talk very much about national identity and mythology and all this, but I used *Bless Me, Ultima* in Buffalo, and these kids have probably never seen many Latino people or Chicano people. Polish working-class kids. They loved the book. They thought it was the best book. It does have universal . . . well, I hate to say that, but it does seem to cut across class and cultural lines.

RA: Well. I think any work of art will. Let me be more specific. I don't write for a culture.

IR: You don't, I see.

RA: It seems to me that would be binding myself. And I don't write for a culture or for a specific political philosophy. I need more freedom than that. Right? The fact that I use all the materials of my culture is very natural. Right? I use the language. I use the names. I use the place here that I know. All that makes sense, but whatever comes out of that in terms of universal experience is, I think, what everybody aims in the creation of a new form. If I sit down and sculpt from a piece of pinon wood a mother with child and I take it to anywhere in Africa or China or Europe, it will be understood. So the fact that I use the wood indigenous to my area, my knife, and I am Chicano with a Chicano thought, doesn't mean that I don't share with every-one else in the world. It's like this book I was telling you about awhile ago, *The Jimbee Bird* by Ismith Khan. It's about this kid growing up in the Jamai-can or the Caribbean islands. It's a universal book. The guy used this lan-guage, folklore, the idea, mythology, historical events. It's a universal book. It can be read anywhere.

IR: Frank Chin and I were talking about this. We all compete sometimes, we're looking for a little attention and to be recognized by Manhattan in all this. In your group, you don't seem to be bothered by that too much.

RA: No. We're not. And that's really interesting. Because when I first published I was brainwashed, like everyone else. I thought that was the way to go and you had to, if not get published by a New York publisher, at least get reviewed in the *New York Times Book Review* or whatever. And one of the things that I think *has* characterized Chicano writers in the Movement is that there has not been that kind of a concern. The more I think about it, the less I care. Sure, if someone wants to review the book, I'll send him a copy. I'm not going to turn it down. I think it's kind of a thinking we have to break down. Just lately, when I finished this workshop this summer, somebody said, 'Well, so-and-so's book got reviewed in the New York book reviews.' That person made the statement as a recognition of quality. And she didn't know that she had done it, but she has been *conditioned* to think once the review is there, it also sets a kind of criteria of quality for the book. That's nonsense.

IR: What do you think of independent publishing in this? They finally had to recognize independent publishing. What was happening for many years was that the big publishers were playing a daisy chain with the big reviews, that they reviewed the big publishers because they get advertising revenue.

RA: Yeah. I think, there's no doubt in my mind, that the reviewing of books is run by the publishers themselves.

IR: Arrange the bestsellers.

RA: You can arrange if you're there to have whatever books you want reviewed. I think we're alternative or underground, at least we're on the fringe of that collective thing back East, and all of our books have to go underground. They have to go by word-of-mouth. They have to go by book-stores that are sympathetic to the literature. They have to be picked up by teachers who are interested, you know, in different ways of thought, different literature. And that's great, because, you know, it means, it really means that people with some sense of what they want to read are reading it. So it's kind of really a good feeling. It's a good feeling, actually.

IR: Let me ask you one last question here. Got a lot of good ones here. There seems to be something that distinguishes the anthologies that I read from out of your books from the average, I don't know what you would call it, the experimental standard of American poetry, confessional poetry, and all that. And one thing I can see is a lot of heart, you know, that we mentioned before, passion. If you had to take this literature, the Southwest, the Chicano literature, what would you say are its main characteristics?

RA: In style, it's hard to pin down now because, I think, not enough critical attention has been paid to the aesthetics of style and form. In the philosophic content of what I have heard and what is making sense to me is that the literature being produced now by the Chicano writer, the Mexican-American writer, is not nihilistic. It has a very positive vein running through it. You *can* be the master of your own destiny. You *can* change the world and create a better place to live. And, *I* think, probably part of that comes from a very hardcore set of values, maybe, that is in the culture itself. That maybe allows you to see, in spite of the oppressiveness of the world, it allows you to see something positive in life. I think that's true because most of the books that I have read deal, they don't deal with only the bright, I don't mean they deal with the bright side of life, everything is a rose garden type thing. Tomás Rivera deals with people that are in the fields, migrant workers who are being oppressed, that are in the worst of conditions. That's a very hard book to read, but you find at the end that the narrator of the book, the main character of the book, overcomes that kind of condition. He will be a better person. He does not slash his wrists or commit suicide.

IR: Okay. It has nothing to do with John Wayne's swaggering. There's a whole philosophy to this, a whole style in philosophy.

RA: Yeah. I think that John Wayne symbolizes the aggressive element in American society. You go into the town and you take it over. Now, that's a statement!

IR: They try to pretend that it's a man-to-man confrontation, but it's usually technology against people without it. You know, California would still be Indian land were it not for howitzers and cannons.

Rudolfo A. Anaya

Juan Bruce-Novoa / 1979

From *Chicano Authors: Inquiry by Interview* by Juan Bruce-Novoa, 184–202. Copyright © 1980. By permission of the University of Texas Press and Juan Bruce-Novoa.

In 1971, the second Quinto Sol Prize for literature brought to our attention a young New Mexican writer, Rudolfo Anaya and his enchanting character, the old curandera [shamanistic wise woman] Ultima, blessed with the magical power and cosmic vision of Carlos Castaneda's Don Juan, without the messianic pretentiousness. *Bless Me, Ultima* became the best selling of Quinto Sol's prestigious titles and still maintains its popularity. Anaya has published a second novel, *Heart of Aztlan* (1976), and his third, *Tortuga,* is in press at the time of this writing (1979).

Following as it did Tomás Rivera's award in 1970, Anaya's winning of the Quinto Sol Prize produced a contrast of Chicano fictional worlds. Whereas Rivera's subject is the migratory farmworker from Texas, Anaya portrays New Mexican families with permanent roots dating back centuries. The sense of space is diametrically opposite: though Rivera's characters wander the country, they always seem fenced in, restricted to small spaces; Anaya's characters feel the limitless expanse of themselves in a parcel of land. The same is true of language and style: while Rivera's is concise, controlled, severely limited to essentials, Anaya's is rich, expansive, profuse. Perhaps the difference can be traced to their distinct experience and the effect of the culture of the area and inhabitants each one knows. Yet close reading of *Ultima* reveals that, in spite of the surface differences and the infinite horizons of Anaya's spatial/spiritual sensibilities, the two novels and the authors share much. Anaya's expansive prose is just as carefully controlled as Rivera's within its fictional ambience. Nothing superfluous is tolerated; Anaya and Rivera—one could add Hinojosa and Arias—are their own best editors. Though at first glance it strikes one as realistic, Anaya's language is ambiguous and evocative. The imagination's power to effect change in the world is central, both thematically and structurally, in both novels. And in the final analysis, both are essentially concerned with the protagonist's acquisition of the ability to see—*read*—the world in its harmonious unity, beyond the superficial divisiveness, and, then, with the need to write what is seen. In each case the novel is the text that proves the success of the apprenticeship.

Ultima produced expectations that *Heart of Aztlan* did not satisfy. Not that the introduction of blatantly political topics is a fault in and of itself—no, it is a matter of the craftsmanship, not of the themes,

11

and *Heart,* for whatever reason, is less polished, less accomplished. Anaya should be admired for having the courage to explore a new space—*Heart* is set in the city—instead of remaining within the circumference of the secure area established in *Ultima. Tortuga,* his third novel, promises to be yet another experiment. Anaya's readers await it with great expectations. *Bless Me, Ultima* assures him a faithful audience.

Rudy Anaya recorded and edited his responses during the winter of 1978–1979.

When and where were you born?

I was born in Pastura, New Mexico, a small village on the llano [plains], El Llano Estacado, which begins in those hills and settles into the plains of West Texas and Kansas, the eastern plains as we know them. It's a harsh environment. I remember most that sense of landscape which is bleak, empty, desolate, across which the wind blows and makes its music. My work is full of references to the land and to the landscape; it can't help but be. I was born in 1937.

The influence of that land was early and lasting. I have tried to describe it in an article, "The Writer's Landscape: Epiphany in Landscape,"* as almost a religious experience, or a religious communication that man has with his earth when the two come to meet at one point and the power which is in each one is energized, no longer remaining negative and positive, but fusing together. That landscape plays a major role in the literature that I write. In the beginning, it is an empty, desolate, bare stage; then, if one looks closely, one sees life—people gather to tell stories, to do their work, to love, to die. In the old days the sheep and cattle ranchers gathered in that small village, which had a train station, a watering station for the old coal-burning trains. It was prosperous; they were good times. Then after the visit or the business at hand is done, the people disappear back into the landscape and you're left as if alone, with the memories, dreams, stories, and whatever joys and tragedies they had brought to you.

Soon after I was born, we moved to Santa Rosa, which was on Highway 66. For me that road was the link between the East and the West. There was much life there. Santa Rosa is a geographical setting, in a sense, that I use to set the stage for *Bless Me, Ultima.* The river flows through the valley, and the highway and the railroad tracks dissect the town in another direction. And

---

*Latin American Literary Review 5, no. 10 (Spring–Summer 1977): 98–102.

always there is the interplay of people on the stage of life with the elements
of nature—and the llano itself working through the people, changing the
people, finally making the people who they are. I can't think of very many
things that I have written that do not have a reference to those natural forces
and that earth and people which nurtured me.

Describe your family background and your present situation.

Family and roots. Everybody is into roots now, since Haley. When people
ask me where my roots are, I look down at my feet and I see the roots of my
soul grasping the earth. They are here, in New Mexico, the Southwest. My
family—the history I know of it—originally settled in the Río Grande Valley
in Albuquerque in the old land grant, which was then called La Merced de
Atrisco, the Atrisco land grant. My great-grandfather was one of the original
incorporators of that land grant. From there the family moved with the first
movement that went eastward into the llano of New Mexico, a recent move
around the middle of the nineteenth century, after it was safe to move out
into those plains. That is where you get some of those small villages along
the river valleys. It was good grazing land for sheep and cattle.

My parents met in a small town by the name of Puerto de Luna, and there
they married and started their family—I have many brothers and many sisters. From the time I can remember, we have always had roots here. I was
fortunate to be born and raised in a small village where everyone knew each
other. The families were related; there were common endeavors. People
worked essentially as ranchers. We owned our own solar—our plot of land
where our home was—and when we moved to Santa Rosa we also owned our
own home. So we always had a firm sense of belonging instilled in us, not
only by the land but, of course, by our parents. The sense of culture, of
tradition, of history was always around us. People told stories when they
came to visit. The elders would sit around the table playing cards or domi-
noes, or just talking, and we would listen to the cuentos. They always talked
about the way things had been, the people who had come here, how families
were related, the old people and what they had done. That filled us with a
sense of pride in our own history, you might say.

I still live in New Mexico. I have traveled to many places, but have no
desire to leave New Mexico. Here I can look around and have a feeling that
these hills, these mountains, this river, this earth, this sky is mine. I feel good
in it. For that I think I am fortunate. I'm presently teaching creative writing

and some courses in Chicano literature at the University of New Mexico. I
enjoy teaching. I'm always working on some project or another that has to
do with writing. I've just finished a manuscript for a novel entitled *Tortuga*
and I'm working on a short story. So every day I meet some collaborator,
some idea, some event, some memory, some sense of the landscape, I hear
something, and I start to write. That's a very healthy position for a writer to
be in. I have time. I have solitude.

When did you first begin to write?

I always answer that question by saying that it was as an undergraduate student, but that's not completely true. I have always been interested in writing.
I wrote when I was a child. I had good teachers who encouraged me to write.
There was always a sense of mystery and awe for me in stories. But I began
to write seriously as an undergraduate student. We had moved to the Barelas
barrio in Albuquerque, but not many of us from Barelas were attending the
university. It was in the late '50s and not too many Chicanos did, but a few
of us were there and we stayed together, forming our own clique—I think we
did it to survive.

We were interested in art: one of us was a painter and a couple of us were
into writing. We read and discussed our early works. I wrote poetry, and I
found that I probably didn't have the gift that some people are blessed with,
and then changed to prose and almost immediately began to write novels. I
wrote two or three novels while I was at the University of New Mexico, on
my own. I didn't attend any writing classes. It was something I felt I had to
do and I wanted to do and was committing time every night to it.

The first two or three novels I think I have destroyed. They were exercises
in learning to write. They weren't worth keeping. Then sometime in the early
'60s I began to work with characters and a story that would eventually evolve
into *Bless Me, Ultima.* I began to tell the story of a family and Antonio, a
young boy, and worked at it for years. It never really took shape, in terms of
inspiration, until the night that Ultima came to me and appeared as a full-
fledged character. She stood beside me and pointed out the things I had to do
with the novel if it was going to work. She suggested that she would be an
excellent character, and worked herself into the novel. From there on it
clicked. It was, of course, the relationship Antonio was looking for.

Between 1963 and 1970 I did six or seven drafts of the novel—complete
drafts. I was still learning to write. It has never come easy to me. I have to

rewrite a lot, trying always, not only for perfection, but for some kind of balance and harmony that will exist in the work when all of the elements of fiction finally are pulled together and work well. Sometime in the very early 1970's, I was reading a copy of *El Grito* from Berkeley, being published by Herminio Ríos, Octavio Romano, Andrés Ibarra, and many Chicano students who had gathered there, and I decided I would send my manuscript to them. At that time *El Grito* was mostly full of California writers and I knew I could write every bit as well as they. So I wrote a letter to Herminio Ríos and I said, look, I've got a manuscript I think you should read. He wrote back and said, let me see it; they accepted it and eventually awarded it el Premio Quinto Sol [the Quinto Sol Prize]. Of course, I was very pleased.

What kind of books did you read in your formative years?

I read a great deal when I was a child, in grade school. I not only ran in a gang and did everything that normal, red-blooded Chicano boys do as they grow up, but I also used to spend a lot of time reading. I was the only one in the gang that used to go to the library on Saturday mornings. It was a decrepit, old building, run by one of the teachers, who volunteered to open it on Saturdays. Many Saturday mornings she and I were the only ones at the library. I sat there and read and leafed through books, and took some home. I read a lot of comic books and saw a lot of movies. I think all of that was important, in some respect, to the question of what influenced me when I was young. I also heard stories. Any time that people gathered, family or friends, they told stories, cuentos [tales], anecdotes, dichos [sayings], adivinanzas [riddles]. So I was always in a milieu of words, whether they were printed or in the oral tradition. And I think that's important to stimulate the writer's imagination; to respond to what is going on around him, to incorporate the materials and then rehash them and make fiction—to start at a point of reference which is close to one's being and then to transcend it, that's important.

Later, I read a great deal in American literature when I was at the university, and it was as formative a period for me as my childhood, because both were very full and alive with the mystery of discovery in literature.

I saw movies, all of the cowboy movies and war movies of the 1940s. The Cantinflas movies were very popular; a lot of Mexican movies were available. So there was a jumble of material there that had an influence in terms of my own writing, there was no one title or work or author that made it click.

What is the extent of your studies?

I received an M.A. from the University of New Mexico in 1968 in English. I had at the time done most of my reading in American literature, influenced, probably, by the Romantics, Whitman in particular, the Imagists, and later by the Lost Generation. I read the poets as well as the novelists. I also was influenced by the classics, Shakespeare, Milton, Pope, Dante. I read a great deal of world literature, philosophy, and religion at that time. Also, it was a very active time of the Beatnik generation. There was a lot of literary activity, new poets, new poetry, coffee shops, and I was listening to it and observing what was taking place.

Has formal education helped or hindered you as a writer?

Of course it has helped me. I was exposed to many writers, not only to American literature and contemporary writers, but world literature. I think it's very important for Chicano students, whether or not they're going to be writers, to engage in some kind of educational process. There are those who say that education will change who you are, how you think, destroy your culture, assimilate you—I think that's nonsense. Those are people who are afraid of change. We cannot hide our heads in the sand and pretend that everything that is important and good and of value will come only out of our culture. We live in a small world where many other cultures have a great deal to offer us. This is very important for the writer—to read as much as he possibly can, to learn a bit of the analytical study of literature. That's important.

Which was the predominant language in your home as a child? Which do you speak more fluently now?

It was Spanish. Both my father and my mother spoke Spanish, and I was raised speaking Spanish in an almost completely Spanish background. I did not learn English until I started first grade. Now I speak more fluently in English. The thrust of my education has been in English literature and I wrote in English when I began to write, so I am more fluent and more comfortable with English.

    Those of us who were raised in a Spanish-speaking environment, knowing the language, loving it, wanting to use it as completely as English, needed help in school to keep the language and develop the skills. We did not receive that help, so now we are handicapped when it comes to using Spanish. It's also happening today. We are going through another generation that is using more English than Spanish. It has a lot to do with the educational system and the little relevance that is placed on teaching the Spanish language in a bilingual setting.

Does Chicano literature have a particular language or idiom?

The only criterion for Chicano literature is that it be written by a Chicano or Chicana. When you talk about language or idiom, you have to remember that the Chicano—historically—is not as tight a homogeneous group as one would imagine, especially in language. We have writers using what we call street language; others use language particular to the Southwest, or, for that matter, to other regions of the country. Some have a particular concern with idiom and it becomes predominant in their work. I suppose you could say that the '60s had a particular idiom. I don't think that's true any more.

How do you perceive your role as a writer vis-à-vis: (a) the Chicano community or Movement; (b) U.S. society; (c) literature itself?

First of all, the role of a writer is vis-à-vis the universe itself, chaos versus patterns. I fit easily and completely into the Chicano community—that's where I was born and raised, that's where my family resides—and the Movement, because I was active in it and have seen its different areas of development. I think that in part I fit into the mainstream society, what you call U.S. society. I know it's fashionable for many Chicano writers to say that they do not belong to this society that has oppressed minorities. Nonetheless, the fact exists that we are a part of that society. I have no trouble at all relating to writers and artists in that society. There are many of its values that I abhor, stay away from, have nothing to do with. But nevertheless, there is a relationship with the creative part of that society that is very valuable for me. I meet its writers, its artists, teachers, and find that we often have a common core of views, goals, and ideas, through broad spectrums that flow from political to sociological to aesthetic.

Since I began writing, or probably since I began reading, I have been hooked into the world of literature, the world of the writer. I very often see myself as a writer first. And why not? As difficult as the endeavor is, as sullen as the craft is, still it has its rewards. It's exciting to be a writer today, to see talented young people interested in the craft and aspiring to be writers, playwrights, and poets.

What is the place of Chicano literature within U.S. literature?

I believe that Chicano literature is ultimately a part of U.S. literature. I do not believe that we have to be swallowed up by models or values or experimentation with the contemporary U.S. literature. We can present our own perspective, and in such a way present to the world the workings of our imagination, filtered through a very long and rich culture. But ultimately it will be incorporated into the literature of this country. The role of the next generation will be to assure that we are not given secondary status, or the back shelves of the libraries.

What is the relationship of Chicano literature to Mexican literature?

Because of the nature of our role in this society, we are tied not only to United States literature, but obviously to Mexican literature. A great many of our writers are very familiar with it because they have studied it, as well as Latin American and Peninsular literature, and have formed a deeper relationship with Mexican literature than with that of the United States. That relationship will continue; it's natural and, I think, good.

In my case, I have not read or studied Mexican literature in an academic setting, but I have read as much Mexican and Latin American literature as possible. I have traveled a great deal in Mexico and I am more familiar with its visual arts. But in the beginning I had the U.S. American novels to work with; I didn't have the Mexican models, so I believe their influence on me as a writer was minimal. But that's only in reference to techniques—the mythology is a different story.

Do you perceive yourself and your work as political?

We can proceed from one cliché, that all work, every act of life, is political, to the other side of the board that says art exists for itself, in and of itself. Somewhere in the middle I would find my place. I have never set out to write a political work. Many Chicano critics find themselves in the Marxist-Leninist camp, where they deride and verbally abuse writers who will not cater to their personal and social needs. What such critics forget is that every man's or woman's creative, imaginative endeavor is an act of rebellion.

The artist is a person in constant rebellion. He does not take rules as they are, nor is he committed to any narrow ideology. He is in constant rebellion with the universe itself. The laws which would provide meaningful patterns to guide and some kind of harmony to exist are constantly being suffocated by chaos. It is out of this chaos that the artist would bring some order, some meaningful pattern, reinstitute some harmony. So it doesn't matter if they are the laws of God, of society, or of our own culture, we are people in revolt, constantly.

I have read some criticism by politically minded people who want to see the art of the contemporary Chicano Movement serve only a social and a political purpose. And more than that, often their own political needs. This is a danger if we are to develop artists. I have spoken against this kind of pressure everywhere. I would like to see other writers do this, writers who are influential and respected, artists—yourself included. You wrote a very interesting piece a long time ago in *La Luz** in which you called for the freedom of expression, which Chicanos must exercise. This freedom will not be given by any political group or any other group of people. The artist will take it in his own hands and rework it as he sees fit. And it will come out in all colors, taking many different directions. There will be some political works, and there will be some that will be concerned with the smallest, most practical details of day-to-day living, concerned with love, joy, and tragedy. That is the kind of freedom we must have, that we make for ourselves as artists.

I caution young artists not to pay attention to critics, especially when those critics want to use them, to use their talents. An artist, to begin with, is a person rebelling against the status quo. He doesn't need any political mentors. An artist should be a person who is far ahead of his political mentors, or he has no business calling himself an artist.

To be quite frank and truthful, I see the effects of politics in the literature. A great deal of the poetry of the '60s was polemic in nature. I myself, when I wrote *Heart of Aztlan,* was very interested in how people take a political system in hand, one that is oppressing and using them. I'm sure Tomás Rivera thought the same when he wrote . . . *y no se lo tragó la tierra.* Perhaps he was not concerned with the system as a study. He has been berated for it. But, my God, all you have to do is look beyond the surface to see that he was

---

*Bruce-Novoa, "Freedom of Expression and the Chicano Movement," *La Luz* (September 1973): 28–29.

addressing political and social questions. He was speaking directly about the menace of political and social oppression. So it comes in different layers, in different ways. It doesn't always have to be up front, shouting in the street. When that is needed, it will be there. That is the trust I have in the artist.

Does the Chicano author have anything in common with the majority group writer? Differences?

There are many writers in the country who desire to know what other regions and groups of people are doing. There is a multicultural emphasis and impetus in writing and in publishing that is very healthy. For example, I work on the board of the Coordinating Council for Literary Magazines and have served on it for five years. In that time I have seen changes. Other writers have become more interested in what Chicanos, Blacks, and women are doing, what is coming out of prisons and different regions. How do we create a truly national literature? How do we break into the literary history that will be written of the '60s and '70s? We do have a lot in common with many groups and we are beginning to work together.

In California, the Before Columbus Foundation is drawing together Black writers, Latin Americans, Chicanos, Native Americans, sponsoring book fairs, readings, interchanges, and discourse. The Turtle Island Foundation is publishing minority group writers very effectively and very enthusiastically. I see a great new generation of Asian American writers coming up in the Northwest, and California, and know some of the writers, Frank Chin, Lawson Inada, Shon Wong, to name a few, all of whom are interested in what we're doing as Chicanos. So that's a very positive development.

It's interesting to note that some of the groups here in the Southwest are exchanging works and information across cultural lines. Even in Texas one of the groups working there to promote literature is making contact with Chicano writers, probably for the first time. That is encouraging. I might add that *The American Book Review,* recently formed as an alternative to the established book reviews, which will not review our works at all, has as one of its reasons for existence to review the literature of minority group writers in different regions of the country. This movement is good, healthy, and I hope it is something we can encourage so that it will stay around.

Does Chicano literature share common ground with Black literature? Differences?

I would have to say that historically it shares many common elements. We're dealing with two minority populations at a time in their history when they both have experienced a surge or a renaissance not only in their literature but in their whole life style and perspective. They have had to deal with values of the majority group which were not their inherent values. The difficulty that both found in publishing and breaking into the publishing field has been great. Finally, the most important is the common shout of identity. I am! The Black writers, especially those who centered around the Harlem Renaissance, had to define themselves vis-à-vis the white world. We have seen that happen in Chicano literature. That, of course, can be a danger. If the literature is only one of defiance of the white world, or only a literature that has an impetus or force as long as that white model exists, then there is a danger, because we cannot define ourselves, or find ourselves, or create our literature only in defiance of that white model. We have to come out of our own experience, our own tradition, culture, roots, our own sense of language, of story, and deal with that and to hell with the white model. You see, I'm saying that we can't just push against it all the time to define ourselves. That is a weakness. We must define ourselves from our own stance. We are who we create.

Is there any relationship with the literature of other Spanish-speaking groups?

What interests me is the relationship among the Spanish-speaking groups within the United States itself. A very interesting coalition could be formed among the Puertorriqueños, the Newyoricans, the Cubanos, the Latinos, and the Latinos, and the Chicanos to begin sharing their work.* I often find that I mention the name of Victor Hernández Cruz to Chicano writers and very few know him. They should. He's a very important Puertorriqueño, New York writer. This relationship, that we should form in terms of readings and conferences, should be encouraged. Just recently, Alurista and Victor Hernández Cruz and a few other Chicanos read at Columbia in New York, and there was a lot of interest, a lot of sharing. That relationship is natural, as natural as the one with Native American writers and the Asian Americans, the Black Americans, women, and regional groups, because the tide is turning in terms of the establishment of literature in the country.

The new emphasis will be, or should be, on a multicultural, a multiethnic literature.

---

*Newyoricans are Puerto Ricans from New York. Latinos here means people of Latin American origin other than Chicanos, Puerto Ricans, and Cubans.

Does Chicano literature have a distinctive perspective on life? What effect does it have on the literature?

All literature, and certainly Chicano literature, reflects, in its more formal aspects, the mythos of the people, and the writings speak to the underlying philosophical assumptions which form the particular world view of a culture. By its more formal aspects I don't mean style, I mean the concern of particular writers for the sense of values which constitutes our world view. This has been a concern of mine as a writer. My interest is not only in the story or the plot of the story but in the presentation *of my vision* of a native American mythology which has permeated our culture with its values. In a real sense, the mythologies of the Americas are the only mythologies of all of us, whether we are newly arrived or whether we have been here for centuries. The land and the people force this mythology on us. I gladly accept it; many or most of the American newcomers have resisted it.

If we as Chicanos do have a distinctive perspective on life, I believe that perspective will be defined when we challenge the very basic questions which mankind has always asked itself: What is my relationship to the universe, the cosmos? Who am I and why am I here? If there is a Godhead, what is its nature and function? What is the nature of mankind? These are basic questions because they form the framework of our relationship with the universe and with each other, and they are questions which, I believe, we deal with on a daily basis as we progress through life. Everyone questions and the mythologies feed some of the answers; the culture acts as a prism which refracts the clear light of the questions and the answer. As our writers and artists and philosophers continue to engage in the exploration of these questions, we will arrive at a closer look at the distinctive perspective. For me, the important thing to remember is that the perspective will be a core of values molded by and guided by culture, history, language, native mythology, and all the other characteristics of the wide umbrella we usually label culture. What we must not forget is that beneath that surface we will find the archetypes and the values and the primal symbols which we share in common with all mankind.

I understand that in the cycle of time, the present time is a time of recognition and flowering of pride, and that is a perfectly acceptable stance. History teaches us that people arrive at times in their history when they look upon themselves as a unique people with a particular role in the politics and social well-being of the world. That may be the first step in the creation of a renaissance. But times of immense hubris or orgullo [pride] can be limiting, not because pride goes before the fall—what the hell, our people have been under for so long that there isn't much room left to fall—but because the time will afford certain writers a crutch. Writers and artists who say they are different only because they speak caló [slang] or because they are brown or because they were raised in poverty (and those criteria apply to most of us) are presenting a very limiting view of the role of art in a society. In slightly different ways, 80 percent of the world fits those criteria, so it's that jump we have to make to understand not only the surface of the damaging circumstances of life but the depth. Art can be a catalyst and a force to assault ignorance and discrimination and poverty and hunger.

Does Chicano literature improve communication between Chicanos and Anglo Americans?

Yes. All art improves communication. Art is communication. I travel around the country extensively, and I have served on national literary boards, for example, the Coordinating Council of Literary Magazines board, and I find that not only are the other minority groups of this country interested in our literature, but the Anglo American who is a serious reader is beginning to read our literature. The influence of Chicano literature is spreading, no doubt. Prejudice against it and the people it represents still exists; my eyes aren't blind to that. Reviews of our work in major journals or book reviews are still nonexistent, few Chicano writers are invited to non-Chicano readings, national private and public fellowships are still denied to us, but in spite of all this there is some change in the air. There is interest in our literature, and that interest is spreading to Europe. In some cases, European universities have undertaken the study of Chicano literature more aggressively than their American counterparts. And there's a new sense of understanding and need for the multicultural nature of this country which is reflected in the literature and art. I believe that the national character of this country will never be known until this sharing of all voices is complete.

Does Chicano literature reevaluate, attack, or subvert the value system of the majority society? Is it a revolutionary literature? Thematically? Technically?

I think I have already answered this when I spoke about my feelings of the artist as a person in rebellion. I have talked about the difficulties that the Chicano and other minority peoples have had in having their literature read and disseminated through the majority society. Is it revolutionary? I addressed that earlier in the sense that all literature is revolutionary, yes. In the sense that we are a small minority struggling for a kind of self-rule, self-independence, yes. But I have also cautioned that it is not only revolutionary literature in the political sense of the word. Its most interesting aspect, what will make it a revolutionary literature, will be whether or not the writers commit themselves to a new literature, one which will mirror or give some intimation of our world view, our values, the core values of our culture.

What problems have you encountered in publishing? Were they racially founded?

This question has probably been answered the same way by every Chicano writer who has tried to publish a manuscript. There are no publishers who are interested in Chicanos as writers. One, they don't know we exist, and two, if they do know, they keep fighting to have us remain invisible. They don't want to see us. And the most racist of them will come out and say that we can't write. I've had this said to me and told to me by other writers. So yes, the problem is there and I've encountered it. I've circulated my manuscripts. In fact, before Quinto Sol was founded and before I knew about it, I circulated *Bless Me, Ultima* and nobody was interested. I think that for a very long time our only alternative will be to publish with Chicano publishing houses. Eventually the problem with that becomes one of evaluation and one of patting ourselves on the back. I think eventually we do have to break out and try other markets.

It's important on the one hand to support and encourage our own Chicano publishing firms because we are a very distinct literary movement, not because we have a literary manifesto. I would argue with many Chicano writers and critics about that. We are a literary movement because of a common social and cultural impetus. I would even argue that we are not a literary movement because of a defined aesthetic. Our aesthetic has been defined by our cultural roots, que son español, indio [that are Spanish, Indian], and whatever we share with the United States mainstream cultural roots. And now we share many things, the most important being language, about which I have spoken. On the other hand, in publishing it does seem relevant to begin to spread ourselves around to achieve this sort of multicultural, multiethnic idea that I talked about earlier. We can't remain in a vacuum; we can't keep reading and teaching our own works and pretend that there is no other literature

around us. We have to be more closely allied with the other ethnic and regional movements that are alive in this country, and begin to send our manuscripts to other literary magazines.

Are Chicanos at a disadvantage in trying to practice the art of writing?

There are some of us who have had, at one time, a great disadvantage. We
came from poor families, poor in the sense that we had no money, but we
were rich with love and culture and a sense of sharing and imagination. We
had to face a school system that very often told us we couldn't write. It did
not teach us our own works, and we had nothing to emulate, to read of our
own. So of course we were very disadvantaged in that way. For example,
when I began to write I had a hard time to find those models that would click,
that had a relevance to my internal being. But I kept at it, I kept at it. You
can call it what you want; it's something you know you have to do, and
eventually you find the rhythm and you find what you want to say and you
say it and you keep practicing the skills and the elements. I don't think they
become any easier, to tell you the truth. After ten or fifteen years now, I'm
still in the process of learning about writing; a process that never finishes.
That's exciting!

Even today Chicano children are being told they are at a disadvantage
because they don't have command of the English language. The sooner you
begin to tell children that, the more they begin to believe it; you build in a
self-fulfilling prophecy. That is not right! We have, as I have stated before, a
rich culture, rich tradition, and rich oral tradition, and we have, through part
of our roots, a rich literary tradition. So we have to change that around y en
vez de decir que no tenemos el talento [and instead of saying that we don't
have the talent], say, "You can write! You do have talent! You can produce
literature that is valuable!" We have to go out and tell the kids in high school
and grade school, cuando están chiquitos [when they are little], "You can
write, you can write about what you know, your experience is valuable, who
you are is valuable, and how you view the world and society and the cosmos
is valuable. Put it down on paper, paint a picture, make a drawing, write
music!" That's the positive way to handle that.

We have to take the arts to kids in the communities and the centers where
they meet, to their families. We've got to desarrollar [develop] the whole
onda [scene], as the current phrasing goes, y que se acabe [and put an end
to] all the negative feelings about the art of writing or the art of anything for
that matter.

What are the most outstanding qualities of Chicano literature? Weaknesses?

For me the most outstanding qualities are that it's exciting and it is experimental. Every new poem, every new novel that comes out is new, is different, it has a new perspective.

Ron Arias's *The Road to Tamazunchale* is a classic. He wrote it as he saw it and it's real; it moves. Orlando Romero's *Nambé Year One* is lyrical. Since I usually am reading or teaching fiction, I sometimes neglect to talk about the poets, but I read a lot of the new poetry and keep up with it. It's also exciting.

There is no written manifesto of Chicano literature. I'm glad no one has attempted to write one. Although some critics have attempted to define the criteria, the limits, the intra-psychology, and the sociological stance of Chicano literature, they have failed, and for that we are a healthier literature.

The weakness has been that we have had writers who are not willing to commit enough time and energy to do their work. It's a craft. When you are not dedicated and you do not take the time to get as near perfection as possible with your work, a perfector of communication, then the work will be weak. I have to continually rework my own manuscripts. *Bless Me, Ultima* was done six or seven times in complete manuscript form, and each one took a year. *Heart of Aztlan* was the same way; I wrote the entire thing three to four times. My current novel, *Tortuga,* I have rewritten three times completely. It's a process that is crucial, unless, of course, you are a genius; then you don't have to rewrite. But I haven't met too many of those.

Chicano criticism? I have been, since very early in the game, a staunch supporter of Chicano criticism. I started teaching Chicano literature some years ago and I wanted the students, in the normal process of looking at any work, to find different perspectives, different viewpoints. How are they led, as you said in one of your articles, how are they led into the work? That's what is exciting about criticism. Everybody has different ways of looking at the work that make the work grow, that make it move, that expand it and create a fuller meaning. I read as much of the criticism as I can get my hands on, and some of it is very good. I think Chicanos have gone out and trained themselves on the par with other critics.

I'm very impressed, for example, with the work Roberto Cantú did on *Bless Me, Ultima.* He wrote extensive critical papers on *Bless Me, Ultima;* whether or not I agree with him is beside the point. The point is that he is valuable for students of literature when they read that novel. There have been some who have done papers of a general nature, yourself included, that have challenged us to look at literary space or the lack thereof. There have been excellent works on individual novels. *Latin American Literary Review* just recently had a special issue that was very good. A lot of it is tough, but it is grounded upon the critics' criteria.

What are the milestones so far in Chicano literature?

I don't know how to answer that question. I think the fact that we are writing, that it is still coming is enough for me. If you mean the works as milestones, go to the people and find out what they are reading. Those are the milestones. What's filtering down to the pueblo, not just staying on the level of the study of literature at the university, but what's filtering down? Where is it being picked up? What's being read on the buses, donde está la gente trabajando [where people work]? There are many works I could name, but again I would rather not get into that. What's exciting for me is that I see the last ten or fifteen years as only the beginning of a movement and that in the next ten or fifteen years we'll see fantastic works. This time we live in is exciting.

What is the future of Chicano literature: distinctiveness, or the de-emphasis of the distinctive characteristics?

The future is bright. The de-emphasis will be on merely mirroring the cultural, in the sense of a representational or realistic mirroring of the culture, the trend is to a more personal work which will carry the culture in it, but will have a concern with experimentation, with style, and perhaps character. Maybe I'm saying this because I feel this is where my work is going. Somehow I never set out to mirror the culture, to hold the espejo [mirror] up to the culture. Many people have said this is what is in my work, but that is not a primary intention of the work. I have always thought that the background—which is the background of my own personal life—will normally fit itself into whatever my concern happens to be. In a sense I think this is repeated in the whole scene of Chicano literature.

I suppose the future will have to include many dramatic works. We have had a history of teatro, the actos. Perhaps now is the right time to experiment with more full-length dramas. Most of the dramas that have been published have been one-act plays. The other thing that I see—and I like it—is the idea of experimentation. A few people come to mind. Joe Olvera, down in El Paso, does absurdist and surrealist things with his work. I think we got a

sense of that in Ron Arias. Perhaps we can even historically date it back to
. . . *y no se lo tragó la tierra* and *Estampas del Valle,* where vignettes and
time points of view changed within structurally small works and helped us
redefine the novel, perhaps even the short story. I see more and more being
written in Spanish. I'm helping to edit, with Antonio Márquez, a short collection of Chicano cuentos [stories] for the *New America* magazine at the University of New Mexico, American Studies Department. We sent out a little
broadside asking for manuscripts and got a big response of stories written in
Spanish. The idea of presenting the work bilingually, I think, will continue,
perhaps even grow. It was an idea started very early by Quinto Sol and the
Chicano writers of the '60's. Of course the form itself has a long history.
When I think of myself and where I'm going, I do not want to sit still. *Heart
of Aztlan* surprised many people because it was not a *Bless Me, Ultima* and
that's what they expected. In fact, you yourself said as much when you wrote
that dastardly review of it. No, no te creas, hombre [Don't believe it], I'm
just kidding you. But you said we shouldn't have expected another *Bless Me,
Ultima* from Anaya, and then you went ahead to say, well, we didn't get one
[he laughs]. Well the point is that we have to be careful to allow writers to
change and to move. Just as *Heart of Aztlan* was different from *Bless Me,
Ultima,* the novel that I'm working on now, *Tortuga,* which has been accepted
for publication and should be out by the time you get this book to press, will
also be different. And people will start asking, ¿qué pasa? what's happening?
What is Chicano in this new novel; is there anything Chicano in it? Change
has to be there. Look at the writers who have not changed, the ones that are
repeating themselves in style and in content. What do they have to say that is
new? There are some writers whose poetry I read in the '60's and I read what
they have published recently, and I say, pues, no cambió [nothing has
changed]. It's still the same material and the same style. We should be aware
of experimentation and encourage it.

Who are the leaders among Chicano writers, and why?

I don't know if I can answer this question in a short amount of time and be
fair to many writers. In fact, I think I won't. It would smack too much of my
own preferences, nothing else. There are too many that I like and that I
admire.

Myth and the Writer: A Conversation with Rudolfo Anaya

David Johnson and David Apodaca / 1979

From *New America*, 3.3 (Spring 1979): 76–85. Reprinted by permission of publisher.

Apodaca: First we wanted to ask you about your personal background. Are the characters in both *Bless Me, Ultima* and *Heart of Aztlan* family people, or are they people that you really know?

Anaya: I was born in a small pueblo—the small pueblo of Las Pasturas right outside of Santa Rosa—which is a pueblo on the llano. I have a lot of very basic types, primal types of memories and images somehow burned into my mind about it—because I lived there only the first year of my life. Then we moved to Santa Rosa. The interesting thing about Pasturas and the llano is that it was a kind of place where I first became aware of the elements. There was space, there was sun, there was wind, there was sky, and there were these people marching across this kind of barren landscape. Very earthy, down-to-earth people, and it seems to me that somehow that got imprinted in my mind. When I did *Bless Me, Ultima* I kept going back to those people that I could first recall as a very, very young child. I was trying to think of them in terms of when I was a year old, what they did to me when I was born, how they affected me when I was in my mother's womb. There were conversations in which I could hear something—or was privileged to in some kind of way. In fact, the more I write, the more I keep going back to developing a landscape that is like that—which is very stark and very bare. It's almost like setting up the barest stage, and people walk across it and they play out their lives, their joys and their tragedies, on it.

Johnson: Are there then actual characters that come out of an early landscape?

Anaya: To me all writing is biographical. It comes out of experience, it comes out of things that you have felt, that you have seen, that you have been involved in; people that you have met, that you have bumped into on this bare stage of life or that you have heard about in stories. And all that became the material for *Bless Me, Ultima*.

29

Apodaca: How old were you when you moved to Santa Rosa?

Anaya: I don't know specifically. I must have been just a year old—two years.

Apodaca: Why did your family move? Do you know?

Anaya: Pasturas used to be, for some of the reasons I state in *Bless Me, Ultima,* a very thriving, central pueblo in terms of the ranching that went on there. There were families that lived there. There was a cantina. There was a big general store that used to be called The General Store where you could buy everything you needed. And then the railroad came in and set up, I think, a water tank. It might also have been a refueling place. So you have the introduction of the railroad. And then, I think, it began to die—because the big ranches came in. You set up bigger and bigger ranches, and the pueblo dies by a kind of natural process of attrition. My father used to work on ranches all his life. And I guess one day he looked around and there wasn't any future in staying in that place, and so he moved. The next step would have been Vaughn or Santa Rosa. We moved to Santa Rosa.

Johnson: We hear about the dichotomy between the people—the Lunas of the valley and the people of the llano. Was that in that area then? A conflict of lifestyles? People who farmed as opposed to the people who ranched?

Anaya: There's a definite difference in lifestyle. In *Bless Me, Ultima* I happened to attribute the lifestyle of the jinete, the vaqueros, to the llanero, which are the Marezes who are tied to the restless sea, the ocean. And the lifestyle of the more passive, more settled Luna to the lifestyle that goes on along the river valley. The dichotomy of a nomadic versus a civilized, settled people.

Johnson: And then the contrast between the sun and the moon comes in at that point—the sun of the llano?

Anaya: The sun is in a sense more restless than the moon, although it has its own cycles. The moon is tied in more to the psyche of the settled farmer.

Johnson: Is Ultima, then, drawn from a real character?

Anaya: Ultima is a character that I never discuss because she can actually be traced. There were women like this; specifically one woman in Pastura, who I think was even related to our family. The interesting thing for me is that I didn't know her at a conscious level when I was old enough to say, "I know this person." But people have since told me, "Well, you wrote about this person," and I say, "No, I didn't remember her, I was too young." And that's where my interest comes in. How soon are we aware of people and the impressions they leave us with? Even when we are not at that very conscious stage of knowing people, but rather the kind of swirl that takes place all around us. People live and die and the tragedies happen. I heard music and the coming together of dances and stories—and then I picked from those. My writing is biographical; I'm not concerned about it being true to reality.

Johnson: Ultima rides a thin line. Although she seems to be on the helpful side as the curandera, nevertheless, she has the kinds of powers that are associated with the bruja, or the black magic. And that line is thin, isn't it, through the novel? Because the people know that she has powers, and they are powers almost outside of the church? Their roots are deeper, aren't they? Almost pagan roots.

Anaya: Well, I think all people are like this. We respond to people of power—in one sense—like the characters in the novel respond to Ultima— with some kind of awe. Sometimes admiration. Sometimes they're thankful for the fact that she can heal them with her remedies, her herbs, her wisdom, her folk psychology if you wish. But the minute that people have power, you also bring another element of response to them. You don't necessarily fear them, but you watch them, create a distance between them, because if they have the power to do wise and good things in terms of healing—physical, mental, or spiritual illnesses—you also wonder do they have the power to create the opposite effect. That's the line that Ultima rides, I think. And she also creates her own distance from people for that reason. She's aware enough to know that that happens to people like her. And so she has no truck with people. If they come to her for help, she'll help, but she also knows that they're a little leary of her.

Apodaca: Then you would say that people who reach that kind of power—in New Mexico to be specific—don't very often get involved politically in their communities. They're more or less isolated. Or do they, at times, become involved politically?

Anaya: They might. But see, we're talking about different types of power. If the ego generates a power that leads a person into the realm or the arena of mixing with people politically and socially, that's a different power. That's charisma. That is more identifiable with the western ego. The kind of power that I think I'm alluding to is different. It's a power that is generated more from the soul or from the sense of being, the sense that you realize that you take your power not from an ego-type of charisma, but a power from what

you have learned from the earth, your identification with the earth—what
you have learned about people and the nature of mankind. That's not specific
to New Mexico, because I have met people from many different places like
that.

Apodaca: I was thinking of Frank Waters' old woman, Maria, in *The People of the Valley.* She is very much like Ultima in some ways, but yet she has
a very large political power it seems. The people don't go to her just for
spiritual healing, or physical healing, but when it comes to points of politics
or counseling even—which often involves politics in their case—they would
go to Maria. That might be more western, or not—the isolated kind of situation that you're talking about—but it's almost from the outside that Frank
Waters develops Maria.

Anaya: When you study the process of self-actualization, you can study it
in various ways. Two ways come to mind. One is you are so conscious and
so aware of yourself—and self-actualized in a psychological sense—that
you're totally aware of yourself in a social situation. You're not paranoid,
you're always yourself and that is often described in terms of social behavior.
But what interests me most in my own life, and in the life of the characters,
is to study that process of isolation of the character. The character being able
to live almost without people, without social setting. Ultima can go and inter-
act. She understands what that social setting is like. But she doesn't need it.
She self-actualizes another way.

Apodaca: What about the other women in your novels? Now you can also
bring in *Heart of Aztlan* if you want. The other women in your novels, com-
pared to Ultima, seem to be very typical women characters. In other words
they're not nearly as strong, or they don't play nearly the kind of roles that
Ultima plays, or the men in *Heart of Aztlan* play. Was this fabricated to be
that way?

Anaya: When I have to develop a woman character, I have a very difficult
time. I look at the earth, I look at life from a male principle. People can argue
that this has primarily been imposed on me socially, but I think that there is
such a thing as a male and a female perspective, a perspective with which
you view the universe, the world. The optimum, or the self-actualized stage,
is to have the male principle and the female principle working in harmony,
like the yin and the yang. And we have that happening in *Bless Me, Ultima.*
Antonio, when we discover him, is both. He's complete. He hasn't broken up
that harmony. One of the things that happens during the novel is that he is

taught more and more about the male character and imbued with that, so that eventually he acquires more of a sense of the male principle.

Apodaca: So it's more balanced when you're a child?

Anaya: It's more balanced when you're a child, and it should be balanced all along, but the way we're taught to grow up, it's unbalanced. And it only begins to be balanced again when you reach an age of conscious reasoning, when you can start looking at this all over again and say "It really shouldn't be that way." Some psychologists, or even some novelists, would say that you're thirty or forty when you begin to try to reestablish your own harmony. It seems to me that I haven't been able to develop, or haven't been interested in really developing strong female characters, because that is *such* a difficult thing to do from my specific given time and male perspective. I'd like to get into it in the future. It would require for me a time of maturation, in order to be able honestly to look at what the female principle is like.

Johnson: How much is it related to the role of the woman in the movement? When we begin to talk about the possibilities for the male character to grow up and look at what he is able to do in terms of his life, is the woman's possibility still more limited and therefore more difficult as a character? Adelita, for instance, in *Heart of Aztlan* doesn't really have the opportunity to do what Clemente does. She really couldn't realistically lead the strike for example.

Anaya: Right. She couldn't lead it simply because of the kind of social and cultural behavioral patterns that are put on male-female, but that's not what I'm talking about. It's only one step to say, "Well, a woman can lead a strike," but it's another role to say, "Why don't we look at people as having a kind of inherent knowledge of both principles to begin with, and never screw them up, never mess them up, so that we only think one way." That's a broader way of looking at an enlightened picture of mankind of the future— when we don't need to worry so much about roles, or even define our individuality in terms of roles. Roles are prescribed by whomever wants you to act in a certain way. Roles are prescribed by forces, by systems. The church and the educational system prescribe roles. Many times the educational system prescribe roles. Many times they never ask if these roles are good for a person or not. They ask are they good for what we want to do with you. So it becomes a kind of pressure. And it seems that the Chicana and the woman outside the ethnic thing are still very, very much hampered by those kinds of roles that have been assigned.

Apodaca: You use the term self-actualization. And in *Bless Me, Ultima* and *Heart of Aztlan* you often talk about the land. And also in a sense about "roots," although I don't know if you used that word. Would "roots," land and self-actualization be synonymous?

Anaya: Yes, because the way in which you self–actualize is by discovering your total environment. Again, we very often talk in modern terms only of being self-actualized with other people. That is, to be congruent with other people. What I am talking about is that there are many more ways which complete the person. A person to me is the pole of a metaphor. Always searching for the other pole. Usually in tension with it. Male in tension with female. You complete the metaphor by dissolving the tension with the other pole, social or communal, finding some kind of a meeting ground. You also complete that by rediscovering the naturalness of the poles and the metaphor of man in his environment. So that if we have been alienated or disassociated or torn apart from the earth itself, to self-actualize you have to rediscover that. You have to also rediscover people, and the female as a principle, the female as a woman.

Johnson: There's this thing of moving into the city, the migration into the city, in *Heart of Aztlan*. And what happens to people who have moved into the city, the sense of losing those kinds of ties to the land, that tend to also lead to the breakdown of the family and to a loss of identity? Is there anything you want to say about what that means? Does it mean moving out of the city, for example?

Anaya: No. Most of the recent statistics I've seen say something like 85 percent of Chicanos are now urban dwellers as opposed to rural dwellers. I don't know if it's only romantic to think about going back and reconstituting the ranchos, the pueblos, but it seems to me that's a most interesting, intriguing question that the novel raises. I say that in modesty because it's already been asked of me; I was in California recently and some of the Chicanos there said, "Well, look, you know you're saying we're a lost generation; we've lost the contact. What do we do?" They were asking the question not only of me, but of themselves. Partly the novel doesn't answer that question, but it's a very important question because it's not just the Chicano, it's all of us.

Johnson: All of us—urban dwellers.

Anaya: Every urban dweller. If he has severed one of those primal connections, that meta-point, and is only one pole of a duality of the metaphor, he is not complete. And how do you complete it? Well, you go around looking for the other pole, and probably there're a lot of answers. One way of answering it is that we must transfer the need for a relation to the earth to a person-to-person relationship. And that means a complete change in the way we look at each other: understanding, first of all, what the relationship meant, and how we can rediscover it. And if not, *then* we're really damned, because then it's every individual to himself, alienated: not only from roots, a connection to the earth, but from fellow human beings.

Apodaca: So in other words, rather than going back to the land in that very direct, literal sense, what you're saying is, recreate a myth and live it or become self-actualized as a substitute.

Anaya: That's the question that I would like the novel, say, to raise, and spark some kind of dialogue.

Johnson: When the characters in *Aztlan* talk about the land, it's almost a mystical use of the land. Where did this come from? It's a religious feeling, isn't it?

Anaya: It's more religious than mystical, I think. Original man was in harmony with his metaphoric setup. And by original I mean a kind of primal sense of understanding the earth without it being mythological or religious or spiritual. You just understood it. You were in touch with it. You gave to it, and it gave to you. There was harmony. Now we call it mythical, because we're so separated from it. It shouldn't be mythical. It's not out there. It's not an abstraction. It's right outside my door. It's in the floor of this room. And if I don't have the sense of harmony to understand myself in relationship to it, then I make it mythical and I separate myself from it, but I don't think that's the way it should be.

Johnson: Do you see that certain people—I'm asking now about the Indians—preserved this relationship in a way, for example, that the Anglo has not? The Anglo in some sense conquered the land, but was not one with the land. Is that part of the tension that goes on in the llano for example? When the big rancher comes in, he doesn't have that feeling for the land. Is there that kind of distinction?

Anaya: I suppose there is. My sense of trying to deal with the earth or the land is not to put that distinction, though, on people. It's more a kind of thing that we should all rediscover about ourselves. Rediscover if we need to. Some people don't need to, you know. Some people have throughout their historic time been very much in touch with the earth, and have never lost it. The empirical reality can be just as screwed up for the Indian, or the Chicano, or the Anglo, as anyone. There's no secret attachment, there's no secret mythology for anyone. I think it's equal for everyone.

Johnson: How does the Indian motif fit into these novels? You invoke it; it's there, but not explained.

Anaya: It's not Indian. It's indigenous. All people at one time are an indigenous people. One way I have of looking at my own work, not so much in process but in retrospect, is through a sense that I have about primal images, primal imageries. A sense that I have about the archetypal, about what we once must have known collectively. What we all share is a kind of collective memory. There was harmony there. It didn't mean it was all Eden. It wasn't like that. The earth is indifferent. It doesn't create an Eden for you, and it doesn't say that collective memory at one time was Eden. It simply says that there was more harmony, there was more a sense that we knew we are dust. That we had been created from it, that we were in touch with it, that we danced on it, and the dust swirled around us, and it grew the very kind of basic stuff that we need to exist. That's what I'm after. My relationship to it. Whatever I am searching for to give more complete meaning to me as a person comes from that sense that part of me in my mestizo nature is Indian or indigenous.

Apodaca: By mestizo, you mean what?

Anaya: Primarily, because I like to deal in dichotomies, because I like to deal in polarities that have to be reconstituted, I mean European Spaniard and American Native. Those two poles trying to come to a kind of harmony in themselves.

Johnson: This leads us then to Chicano, and where that fits in. Is this part of how you see your role as a writer? That is, rediscovering that tension, that body of belief for the Chicano?

Anaya: Not for the Chicano. For myself.

Johnson: Is there a larger role for these works in terms of a people or a region? Or isn't this part of your consideration?

Anaya: I don't know how much of a consideration it can be when you're writing, when you're creating any work of art. I don't think that most artists think in terms of the overall, the world view. It flows from within, it flows

from the individual, and it flows into whatever particular work of art you are
into.

Johnson: But outside the actual process of creating the work, aren't you
somehow asked by the community to be something more? As the author of
Bless Me, Ultima, doesn't the movement itself make demands, ask you to
play a *role as a writer,* not just as a creator?

Anaya: It's true that the Chicano literary movement of the '60s and '70s
has looked at its writers, and the artists in the plastic and visual arts, to begin
to give a picture, or to present the sense of the overview. What are we as a
people? I don't think the artist should get caught up in that. I think any kind
of description or dictation to the artist as a creative person will ruin his
creative impulse.

Apodaca: Then you don't have any feeling of responsibility towards the
people—the Chicano people, or the Chicano movement? One critic said that
he felt that *The Heart of Aztlan* really failed in a certain sense, because that
responsibility was not there on your part. Because there were things in the
novel that were not of the times or of the Chicano movement, and therefore
they didn't contribute to that movement, or to bettering the life of the people
in any way.

Anaya: You have to reword that, because for one thing I'm not concerned
with what critics say, or with their response to my work. If I get concerned
with a critic, then what should I do, write for that critic? That's just like
being prescribed to by anyone else. Your responsibility in the end is totally
your own. If somebody says you failed in it, that's the way he sees it.

Apodaca: I was just stating that someone had felt that you should have
some responsibility in your work towards the people in the Chicano movement. Of course, you said that you don't feel that way.

Anaya: I can't say that I'm totally unaware of a responsibility that I might
have towards the movement, towards my people, towards myself as part of
an ethnic group. Of course I'm aware of it. The writers are the ones that
usually get asked the question, "why don't you be responsible, why don't
you write about the people and the real settings?" and so on. "Why mess
around with the magical realism trip that you get into with *Ultima?*" I'd like
to see the same question asked of Chicano leaders, Chicano musicians, Chicano middle class people, Chicano scientists, Chicano doctors, Chicano lawyers. Nobody ever gets tagged with that really heavy question except the
writers.

Apodaca: Maybe it's because writers are published, and their creations are spread out so far.

Anaya: But, you see the kind of pressure that it puts the writer. It's a very, very difficult type of pressure to deal with, and it's especially difficult for writers who are beginning, who are really young, who want to say, "I want to express myself from my viewpoint, from wherever I'm coming from, from what is important to me, as opposed to that responsibility someone puts on me from out there." I think it can ruin a writer. The best writers will deal with social responsibility and the welfare of the people indirectly—as opposed to a direct political statement or dogma.

Apodaca: Both of these novels, *Bless Me, Ultima* and *Heart of Aztlan,* are the kind of work that after I have read them I immediately wanted to turn around and give them to somebody in La Raza, say my father or my aunt—and they aren't necessarily people who read books. They read newspapers, they read very little, but I had the feeling that they would pick up this book and get a tremendous amount out of it. And on the opposite side, of course, you have the literary critics, the educated who are reading the novel maybe for an entirely different reason. But it does seem that your novels reach out further than many literary works do. There are a large number of people in the barrios, and so on, who don't normally read, but they hear about the novels and will pick them up. In that way the work is influencing the movement or the people.

Anaya: But where I part company is that . . .

Apodaca: You won't tailor the work?

Anaya: I won't tailor the work, and I can't be responsible for the influence. The responsibility is there because we all share this planet. The paradox is this: if I say I take responsibility only for myself and for my actions, it sounds selfish, it sounds egotistical. I'm willing to stretch that and say that in taking ultimate responsibility for my own actions and my own creation, I therefore take responsibility for everyone in all of the universe. Do you see what I mean? People don't get past that paradox. When you say you're only responsible and interested in your own creation, they immediately stop there and they say, "Aha! you're creating art for art's sake." What a limited view! Every action, everything I do, not only affects the universe, but I'll take it a little bit further and say with every moment that I live I am creating a universe. If there is morality or immorality, or good and evil in the universe, I am creating it.

Apodaca: In your dealing with myth—whether it's with Ultima or with the Aztec myth in *Heart of Aztlan,* do you see yourself as creating, re-creating, the myth? Or as simply using myths and symbols that are already there?

Anaya: I see myself more in the process of re-creation. Because I'm not interested in telling or adhering to any myth and being truthful—in the sense that you research and really try to understand the myth. Man is a myth-making animal and this is one of our failures as modern man. We're not making myths anymore, and it interests me in writers that I read and in my own work to make myths; and not only to retell a myth, but to take bits and pieces and remake it with a modern meaning that says something to our lives now. So the myth of the migration of the tribes that passed through this country—then travelled in Meso-America and the Valley of Mexico and its environs—interests me only because of the bits and pieces that strike a chord in that kind of memory that I have about what happened. Then I take bits and pieces and re-create them like I did in *Heart of Aztlan.* The merging of the eagle and the serpent in the mythology of the Aztecs because Quetzalcóatl, the plumed serpent. It became the merging of polarities; it became the drawing down of the highest power that there is, that is closest to God, that aspires to the heaven, with that power that is closest to earth. You merge the two. What if we then create a snake that is like the train, that is the snake of steel? And then Clemente takes on the aspects of the new bird, the man who can fly, and he must come down and wed those principles again. If you leave them separated, if you leave a polarity or dichotomy, then the world is going to destruction. So it seems to me that we have to look at that principle that is throughout all cultures and throughout all mythology, and say, what does it mean to us?

Johnson: So it's not so much that the myth is a myth that has to be in some sense true outside the novel, but the primary thing is this wedding of tensions. That can happen outside the novel even though the actual myth might be slightly different.

Anaya: Right.

Johnson: When you think, for example, of asking where is Aztlán? Aztlán becomes the person who weds them, is that it?

Anaya: It's an attempt to give, a modern sense, of ourselves as myth-makers, as opposed to people who only hear ancient myths and wonder what the hell they're about. You see, if we look at all the ancient myths of the world and we assume that only at one phase of mankind we made myths, then we're in trouble. But if we say, we too are myth-makers, because the myth has at its core a very basic type of human imprint, or symbol.

Apodaca: But isn't it necessary to actually live the myth, rather than to just write it and read it?

Anaya: In writing it, I live it. I encounter myself in the myth, and for me it's a tremendous process in terms of learning about myself. The reader also takes from the arts, or from whatever sources are available, and uses the myths. The myths are a way of getting in touch with yourself, your real essence, what you really think of your nature.

Johnson: One of the things that's interesting about the Aztec, and use of that material, is the tremendous amount of violence that was associated with those original materials. Doesn't it relate to motifs in the barrio? We see Clemente pounding on the steel. What about violence?

Anaya: In terms of mythology, we also see Beowulf pounding on Grendel, and savagely and violently destroying a part of his own reflection. We can go on and on. I think we have to separate the two. It is not the violence of the myth that gets translated, necessarily, into a modern setting in which we live. The violence of the barrio is a reaction towards oppression. When you are shut off from being who you can most completely be, you strike out. When you can't be a doctor; when you can't be a scholar; when you are trapped by forces that tell you you have a limited way of expressing yourself, a limited way of being, you have a limited essence. Everything that is natural to you as a person, as a human being, rebels against it; you strike out.

Apodaca: Why did you pick the Quetzalcóatl myth for *Heart of Aztlan?* Is it because of what you mentioned before, the unity that you're trying to establish? There could have been other myths, I'm sure.

Anaya: The Quetzalcóatl myth is the most basic one to the mythology of Meso-America. It's the primal, the overriding myth. How do you wed the highest aspirations of man with the earth? How do you wed God and the snake? The eagle that represents the aspirations toward the sky-head—and the understanding of that kind of unity—with the unity that the earth itself gives you? Knowing that you are part of both, both polarities again.

Apodaca: Do you think you have to have any justification for this myth sort of popping up in the middle of the barrio, and becoming so important? For Clemente, who came from some place else entirely, and obviously all these people in the barrio. Did they know anything about Quetzalcóatl as such, in a historical sense, or in an educated sense?

Anaya: It is important to know it in an historical sense; it's important that people are literate about their own literature, their own historical background, but myth is a level beneath the literate level. It operates all the time, and you can be separated for a hundred years, for two hundred, for four hundred, for a thousand years, from what is essentially your mythology, but the separation is a veneer. The myth will always emerge. It has to surge out and be known, because you carry it with you.

Apodaca: Is that true for the Anglo as well? This particular myth?

Anaya: Yes, because this particular myth is universal. It's Christ the man also being Christ the God, the plumed serpent. It's having all the powers of godhead and yet being composed of the clay of the earth, of the dust. And how do you reconcile them?

Johnson: There are almost magic elements in the *Heart of Aztlan,* Crispin and the guitar, the woman with the piedra mala. Can you talk about those supernatural elements?

Anaya: The blue guitar is not supernatural; the blue guitar is a symbol in a sense, or an emblem, of a voice of the poet. The poet will sing, the poet will speak. The priest or the philosopher will speak. It's interesting that in the third manuscript the blue guitar gets passed on. You have to have a poet that will dig to the level of myth and speak the truth, not only of that substratum level of myth but about his reality, and then tie the two together.

Johnson: But that person is not necessarily the leader. That merely is passing on the tradition.

Anaya: Passing on the tradition. It could be the cuento, the oral tradition, the stories, the myths. The other part you asked about was the rocks. That's something else that I really worked with. The power of Quetzalcóatl is the power of the blending or the merging of the dichotomies. These polarities of God and earth, of spirit and flesh, cooled off, cooled and congealed into rocks. La piedra mala is the congealing of this force into a rock which the poet, or the writer, has to reinfuse with life and mythology for the sake of mankind, for the sake of people. Rocks contain our history; they're almost a way of going back to my collective memory—if I want to know what happened in this land 20,000, 40,000 years ago. If we can decipher the story in the rock, we can decipher our own memory, our own history. There's even a scientific explanation for that, if you want to carry it a little bit further. Given a certain amount of radiation and energy that rocks give off, some day we'll be smart enough to put a machine next to a rock and decipher the history of the earth.

Johnson: Is there anything you have to say about the problems that the writer has when he tries to deal with that kind of material?

Anaya: For me it has been a very enlightening process. Writing for me has revealed more and more of who I am. And at the same time, it's psychologically and physically very difficult. Any time we engage in the process of knowing who we are as completely as we can—given our limited apparatus—and really dive into the rock, we run into all sorts of edges where we might step off and never come back. I run into that sense of, how far can I go. How do I separate the reality of myself vis-á-vis the rock over there as opposed to this complete blending?

Johnson: Are there influences—books, writers—that feed into this growing process, that have been important to you in terms of the process of incorporating these kinds of materials and ideas?

Anaya: There're just too many to talk about a specific literary influence. It's more the kind of influence where you take all of life, not only writers, but back to that stage I talked about earlier where you think about people you have known, the people that came across the Llano and stopped at our home and visited and gathered me in their arms when I was a child and kissed me and held me and told me stories. The influence is so broad.

Apodaca: Did you do any research for either of the novels?

Anaya: I don't like research. I think research is harmful to the writer. It's not harmful to a presentation like a Michener makes. He can go out and research material and then put it in his own words and incorporate it in a story, but for my search for who I am and the story that I want to tell about those findings, I don't think research is needed. In research you wind up telling somebody else's story or somebody else's idea.

Apodaca: You explained about your background, the movement from Las Pasturas to Santa Rosa; how did you get here? Did your family make another move or was that on your own?

Anaya: Yes, we moved from Santa Rosa to Albuquerque.

Apodaca: How old were you then?

Anaya: I guess about fourteen, fifteen.

Apodaca: Did your dad come to work on the railroads?

Anaya: Writing is biographical but it's not autobiographical. The kind of translating that you do from your history to the page is not exactly as it happened. It can't be.

Johnson: What about Clemente and his awakening? That's a difficult part of the novel in terms of making it believable.

Anaya: It's the most difficult, because he's caught up in a very realistic setting and then how in hell do you take him into this visionary trip that I attempted to do with Clemente. It's very difficult, especially the way I did it. I suppose I could have done it in a dream, I could have done it in some kind of revelation, and I chose to do it instead through Crispin and the old woman, the keeper of the rock.

Apodaca: Do you think the revelation that Clemente comes to works in the novel?

Anaya: I'm no longer concerned with whether it worked or not. It worked for while I was doing it. And I had a final manuscript and that was it. If I look back at it now, or if I look back at it in twenty years and I say, by god, it didn't work, it's of small importance as long as I go on and do another work which might work better.

Johnson: Do you want to say something about the act of writing? Are there things that a young writer needs in order to go about the process?

Anaya: I think anybody who writes should just write the hell out of everything, and not be concerned with the other things we get concerned with. When writers begin to write they often get concerned with publishing, things like that. I don't think that's a concern of the writer. What do other people think of it? That's not the concern of the writer. He or she can get help from other people. It's very important to get good editorial help, somebody that'll really take a heavy look at what you're doing and give you a lot of constructive, hard criticism.

Apodaca: Who did this for you?

Anaya: My wife.

Johnson: What about your publishers?

Anaya: My publishers, the two that I have worked with, have done very, very little editing of my work. I've had to present it as is. In other words, *Bless Me, Ultima* and *Heart of Aztlan* are as is, the way they were when I did them. Herminio Rios helped me with my Spanish, which is rusty. But in terms of major editing, like here you should develop another character, or this character needs this real hard core editing—it was already complete when I sent it in. Someone who submits a first manuscript should get an editor that takes an interest in it. If you have to spend another year or two on it, spend it, because usually if you're working with people who know the business, it's for the best.

Apodaca: The kind of editing you're talking about, I tend to associate with the larger publishing houses. Would you classify the publishers of your two novels as small press publishers?

Anaya: Yes. Definitely.

Johnson: Do you have feelings about how you would like to see your work published in the future? Would you like to see your work in a larger house?

Anaya: Yes and no. Quality will eventually be known. While I know that poorly written work can be sold to the American reading public because of the media and the kind of money that publishers can put into selling, I still have a gut feeling that people who really create and are interested in literature will eventually look for the best, the quality.

Johnson: But isn't there the problem of distribution and promotion that the larger publisher takes for granted?

Anaya: Yes and no. Some big commercial publishers will take a work and do a 2,000, 3,000, 5,000 edition and do nothing at all for it.

Johnson: You've mentioned at various times that there's something positive about supporting the publisher that backed you earlier by saying, "This is something we believe in." Is that still part of your thinking?

Anaya: Yes, especially because Chicano publishing houses in my case began to publish Chicano writers and that's how many of us got published. I think we have felt loyalty, because they helped us. The next step, which is already here because there're Chicano writers publishing with all sorts of publishers now—the next step is that the Chicano publishers will establish themselves well enough so that we don't need that kind of relationship forever.

Apodaca: So that you can break away from the Chicano publisher?

Anaya: So you don't have to feel that sense of staying in one place. And I would hope that that would come very quickly, because the Chicano publishers cannot publish all that's being written. The new writers will have to go to other publishers elsewhere.

Apodaca: What about what other Chicano writers are doing? What do you think of their work?

Anaya: I'd rather not get into that. There's just too much work; there's damn good work. Whatever started in terms of a literary movement is still very much alive and it's producing new works all the time. You know some of the works that have come out, Ron Arias' *Road to Tamazunchale,* Orlando Romero's *Nambé Year One.* Whether or not writers like that see themselves as Chicanos or in the movement somehow doesn't matter. The work is coming out. Tomás Rivera has a new book; Rolando Hinojosa has a new book; Joseph Torres-Metzgar has a new book, *Below the Summit.*

Johnson: What about techniques in your writing? Is there anything you want to say about that? Either the procedure that you go through or from the standpoint of what you've studied?

Anaya: I'm very interested in setting up a kind of universe of people and characters and place around which I could do all of my writing. I'm very interested, obviously, in myth; I'm very interested in symbol and how it works. I'm very conscious about plotting symbol, of using it. I get a kick out of doing things that I know people will respond to, especially critics. In *Heart of Aztlan* I did something that was really maybe too cutesy. Here, I'll read it. It starts with the italic which is the extra reality type of story that's going on in this book, as opposed to being told in dreams and mythology as in *Bless Me, Ultima.* This is done with a sense of you don't know who the narrator is that's dropping this:

> The sun sucked the holy waters of the river, and the turtle-bowl sky ripped open with dark thunder and fell upon the land. South of Aztlan the golden bear drank his fill and tasted the sweet fragrance of the drowned man's blood. That evening he bedded down with the turtle's sisters and streaked their virgin robes with virgin blood.
>
> Oh wash my song into the dead man's soul, he cried, and soak his marrow dry.

That's part of that. I get carried away.

> Let his eyes burst like dying suns and let his blood sweeten my fields of corn.

I'm very interested in the resolution of the body and soul, the body into becoming the things that we eat again and the soul into the winds of the universe, which is the sense I have of the oversoul or what we go to.

The deep water of the canal had dumped Henry in the river and the muddy current of the fish-thumping river sang as it enveloped its burden. It was a high river that bore the body southward—

So that if he drowns in Albuquerque it's going to take him south, right?

—toward the land of the sun, beyond succor, past the blessing of las cruces, into the desolation that lay beyond el paso de la muerte.

I planted it, right? Socorro, Las Cruces, El Paso. That's what we're talking about. I like to play around with names of characters; for example, Ultima, the last, the last one. But earlier you mentioned something that I wanted to talk to you about. We were talking about the axes, the North-South, East-West axis. I'm very interested in the sense of direction in *Bless Me, Ultima,* and that it's obviously an archetype—you pointed that out to me. But did you ever carry it to this? The East-West axis is a western axis; that is, it starts on the East coast from a European source, and comes . . .

Johnson: The westward movement.

Anaya: And the North-South is the other migration, the Asiatic migration through the Americas down south. But in terms of psychologies or world views again, can we attach a psychological frame of reference to the two axes? Is the East-West axis fundamentally a Freudian axis, and a way of explaining everything that we do as human beings through sexual impulses, as opposed to a North-South axis that always is looking for a reconciliation of what we talked about earlier, the eagle and the serpent? It sees a polarity but it also sees a unity which the East-West axis doesn't provide us.

Johnson: I see the East-West axis—and this fits in with Freud—as being the problem of the individual.

Anaya: And you also have individual—communal.

Johnson: Exactly. So you go to the East if you want to save yourself. In other words, having gone as far west now as we can, we now look back to the East, but it's the East for individuals, to save their own souls. You take up Zen, or whatever. And it's the North-South axis that is beginning to talk about the sense of the community being healed.

Anaya: Well, all of Chicano literature, or a great deal of it, is talking about the reconciliation of self within the community, within the communal self, which is exactly what Jung says. You rediscover who you are individually in your collective memory, not in your individual memory. It's Freud who hung us up with the individual memory.

Johnson: You're not whole until the community is whole.

Anaya: And not only that but, take it further, diagram it; you have a graph, and you come up with . . .

Johnson: The cross.

Anaya: Or the tree of life, and the question is, can these two meet, and you not only have what each one presents as a world view, but you have again two polarities that can be reconciled and point to a new kind of way.

Johnson: And when you take that North-South axis seriously, then we are in Aztlán, we are the borderline between the two, the meeting place, the cusp. That is, this whole region.

Apodaca: Where do you feel your roots are? Are they in the mythology you're talking about, in Las Pasturas, in the mestizo, or are they just in the land?

Anaya: Well, I think they're primarily in the land, and in the collective memory; in the collective sense of who I am, with both of the axes. Because if I am mestizo, I share in the East-West axis. But I'm more aligned on the North-South axis; for the total sense of me as a communal person, I have to find the point where they meet. They almost become the eagle and the serpent again. East-West-North-South: how do we wed them together?

Johnson: Where does your work go from here? David thinks there's a trilogy.

Apodaca: I see Antonio in Jason. As Jason is an older Antonio, and then for the third part of the trilogy I want to see an older Jason. Could you say something about the third part of the trilogy?

Anaya: The manuscript that I'm working on now, which will be the third part, will take one of the characters from *Heart of Aztlan* into an environment that is as bleak and as stark as this little village on the llano. And it will deal with the kind of crippling of life that we have created in our society, where love is no longer the predominant feeling that we have for one another. Once love is not the feeling that dictates our social interaction with each other, then we cripple people, and we create outcasts, aliens, and that's what I'll be looking at in the third work.

Apodaca: Do the myths play a large part in the third book?

Anaya: A different kind of mythology. It won't be like the golden carp or like the myth that Crispin tells Clemente.

Johnson: What did you say at the beginning about creating a place?

Apodaca: That you would create an environment, essentially, where all of your work would move in that same environment, all of the characters?

Anaya: Somehow it's coming that I'm working not only my way out of words into silence, but my way out of complex environment or place into the most essential element. I would like to go back and do some dramatic work that is set in nothing but an horizon where there are little adobe houses. All the tragedies that we know can take place there.

Johnson: That's interesting, stripping away some things . . .

Anaya: Stripping away everything. And as you strip away everything you go back to that kind of thing I was talking about earlier. What did these people say when I was a child, what did they tell me about their lives and in their stories? The cuentos they told mother and father. And you strip away everything and get a different kind of environment to come from.

An Interview with Rudolfo Anaya

Jim Harris / 1979

From *Southwest Heritage,* 11.3 (Fall 1981): 16–19.
Reprinted by permission of publisher and Jim Harris.

This interview was conducted two years ago, Mr. Anaya answering questions on tape.

Harris: How long have you been writing? How did you get started?

Anaya: I have been writing since I was an undergraduate student at the University of New Mexico in the late 1950s, early 1960s. The process has been long and laborious because I had to teach myself so much of the craft of writing. Why I got started, why any writer gets started is the most difficult question on earth to answer unless of course you say, I wanted to make money, which doesn't fit me. That's not why I began to write. I think I felt I had a story to tell. I knew that out of the experiences, incidents, people, dreams and the recollections that I had had as a child growing up, as a young man, were somehow important enough to put down in story form. So I started writing novels. And because the novel allowed me more space and freedom, I very quickly adopted that genre, or maybe it adopted me. Who knows?

Harris: Do you think of yourself as a regional writer? If yes, in what sense?

Anaya: Yes, of course. Who isn't a regional writer? Every writer writes, in part, out of the experiences in his life, out of the places and people that he has known and which have moved him to recreate their stories. Somehow the tag of regional writer has always had a negative connotation to some critics and to the academics. I think it's nonsense. Out of every region, out of every person's experience, out of each heart, out of each soul, we expand regional material into that communication with the outer world which then acquires another label. It is then called universal. You have universalized the experience, but it seems to me most people start with very intimate stories, very intimate experiences. I'm obviously affected by the region in which I was born. I have used this as a setting, as a background in my novels. It and the people have influenced me very much, and in that respect I am a regional

49

writer. And I see nothing negative at all about the label. It's a label that shouldn't be used when we think about the creative process. It seems to me that the creative process is always an impulse to recreate life, to recreate inner experiences. Region just happens to be the backdrop that is used. I think, often, the more that region, and by this I mean not only landscape but people and customs and language and mores and mythologies, the more it infuses a work the more that work is universalized. There is no paradox to that for me.

Harris: What is the function of the novel and the novelist in America today?

Anaya: To keep writing novels. I don't know if I can add much more than that. If you mean by that question if there is a special function in which the novel should be analyzing social and political and economic developments and perhaps be pointing toward a direction of the future, analyzing the social fabric of not only regions but of people and of the country itself, then the answer is that novels have been doing that for as long as they have existed. If you mean by that, should the novel enter a new era in terms of innovation, of course that's being done. So the question is unclear to me in the sense that the novel functions as much for the reader, the society, as it functions for the novelist and the particular use he makes out of that art form.

Harris: What writer has influenced you the most?

Anaya: I never answer that question. No one writer has influenced me. I cannot point to one writer and say this is why I am writing, this is what I write like, this is what I would like to emulate, this is the writer that really turned me on. Instead, I think that the opposite is true. Many writers have influenced me. Primarily, the modern and post-modern American novelists and poets, a few of the Latin-American writers, the classics, some Eastern writers. It seems to be that the influences are from many sources. In fact, the sources are so diverse that a true answer would have to reflect what did you read in grade school or before you were in grade school, the comic books you were reading, how you were influenced by the movies. In my case, how you were influenced by the oral tradition, that is, the stories that are passed down generation after generation in the Southwest. In my case they have had a great influence on my work, and have infused themselves into the work and into my life and into the re-creation of a philosophic stance or a world view that my characters take.

Harris: What is the source of your work? Place, people, ideas?

Anaya: I think, I have already answered that. Primarily the background for *Bless Me, Ultima* was the llano of eastern New Mexico, in and around Santa Rosa. I was raised there. I used the town as a setting. I fictionalized, I changed. I used people I knew as prototypes. I used stories that I heard as a child growing up. And in a sense I used the mythos or the mythology of the people. That's been a very, very important and a rich source for my work. But the sources somehow are only the impetus or the beginning of the work. What I was trying to do in *Bless Me, Ultima* in *Heart of Aztlan* and in *Tortuga* is not only use the background or general idea I had of people and experiences, but use that as a takeoff to recreate the story and character's own way, allow him or her to recreate the story. Then I should delve into the more primal, essential mythology that would reflect the world view of my heritage and my culture. And in the end would reflect my own philosophy of life, one would say.

Harris: Has the publication of *Bless Me, Ultima* influenced your writing?

Anaya: Yes and No. How shall I explain? Obviously, every writer is influenced by the publication of his first work. In my case it was a first novel which met with very positive responses and received quite well, in spite of the fact that it was published by a small press that has not the money to indulge in the type of nationwide advertising that bigger presses can do. I have been very pleased with its success, the responses that people have to it. But I know that I couldn't stop there, I couldn't write another *Bless Me, Ultima,* I couldn't write for that matter a sequel which many people asked for. I had to keep growing by changing characters, location, changing themes, changing concerns. That's why I tried what I did in *Heart of Aztlan,* the second novel which is set in a city, the barrio of a bigger city, like here in Albuquerque. And that's what I tried, what I did in the third one, in *Tortuga.* It seems to me that it would have been a mistake for me to have tried to repeat in any shape, manner, or form *Bless Me, Ultima.* It would have stifled whatever growth I had to do in terms of learning the techniques of the novel itself and in terms of progressing with other characters. The influence has been positive of course. I have never regretted it. It's been very good, but I hope that I can be truthful with myself and I say that I still want to keep growing and go to other things. Sometimes it's very difficult when a novelist receives success with a first novel. People expect repeats. Of course it's unfair to the writer, and the writer should be wary of it and not stay there. You have to keep growing.

Harris: Would you comment on the structure or shape of *Bless Me, Ultima?*

Anaya: So much has been said about the structure or shape of it. There are several papers that I could quote that have analyzed the time structure, the flow of time, the structure of the dreams and how they work in and out of the novel. I suppose if I were very truthful and could go back to a point when *Ultima* was taking shape, I would say that the structure was rather organic in a sense that it was growing as it went. I was obviously concerned a great deal with the way that time played in and out of Antonio's world, of the characters that came to shape his world, the things that he had to see. I don't suppose a writer can separate completely what is conscious in terms of the symbols and motifs that he is working with, the threads of the theme that weave in and out of the novel. We are never, when we allow a work to grow organically, aware of what parts of it works out subconsciously. That in *Ultima* was very, very important to me, and I think governed a great deal of the shape it took.

Harris: As a writer, what was the crucial episode in the development of Tony, the protagonist in *Ultima?*

Anaya: Antonio is the young boy, the young child that we meet in *Bless Me, Ultima* at the beginning of the novel, and since it's first-person narration we follow him through his adventures to the end of the novel when Ultima is murdered. I don't know which was the crucial episode. I think if the novel is episodic in part, then each episode should blend or build up the vision that Antonio eventually has to see. To my way of thinking there is no one episode that opens his eyes. His eyes are partially opened on page one when he meets Ultima and he can see the beauty of the land that surrounds him. His eyes are opened when he confronts the dogma of the church. His eyes are opened when he encounters the death of people he loves. His eyes are opened in his dreams, in his contact with the gang, the young kids in the town, in his vision of the golden carp. So, that it seems to me that instead of a crucial episode there are many episodes that open Antonio's eyes until in the end he can begin to see, or perhaps see a glimmer of the truth which Ultima wanted him to see, and that is the holistic nature of the universe, to see beyond the dualities that at first are very apparent to him and those people he comes in contact with. Ultima continually asks him to see beyond that, to incorporate those dualities into a vision that is whole and into a vision that is complete.

A Dialogue: Rudolfo Anaya/
John Nichols

Kevin McIlvoy / 1982

From *Puerto del Sol,* 17 (1982): 61–85.
Reprinted by permission of publisher/Kevin McIlvoy

Rudolfo Anaya is currently revising a collection of short stories which will include a section entitled "Notes On Writing," an opportunity for the author to discuss writing process, storytelling techniques, influences, and other subjects. *Rosalinda,* a screen treatment he is writing for the Corporation for Public Broadcasting, is also almost finished, and he has begun a new novel set in Albuquerque. In the coming year some of his work might be translated into German and Portuguese by various small presses.

John Nichols, who hopes to begin soon a long epic novel about the rise of industrial capitalism in the United States from about 1865 to the present, is working on several film projects. He rewrote the screenplay for the just-released movie, *Missing,* directed by Costa Gavras and starring Sissy Spacek and Jack Lemmon. He has agreed to create a film for Costa Gavras, the director of *Z* and *A State of Siege,* about nuclear scientists. His screenplay of *The Milagro Beanfield War* is being considered by directors Moctezuma Esparza and Robert Redford, while director Louis Malle has accepted his script of *The Magic Journey.* This August, Mr. Nichols' newest book, *The Last Beautiful Days of Autumn,* will be published.

The dialogue which follows was taped in Rudolfo Anaya's home in Albuquerque, New Mexico, on January 22. In order to participate, John Nichols took upon himself the inconvenience of driving from Taos to Albuquerque and, four hours later, back to Taos. Discussion, which centered around subjects, began at 4 p.m. and did not end until 9 p.m. The authors addressed themselves to each topic with genuine enthusiasm and care, politely asking me time and again if they had exhausted the topic at hand before undertaking the next.

Mr. Nichols was constantly animated. Punctuating his speech with "Right? Right?" he would answer his own question by having another stab at the same topic and another yet until he was satisfied he had spoken his mind to his liking. Always leaning over the table he and Mr. Anaya shared, he gestured pointedly and frequently. Mr. Anaya, who kept his hands on his knees, usually leaned back in his chair and, if his own response did not satisfy him, drew on his cigarette or scraped the ashtray before him with a butt before trying again. In instances of disagreement, they unhesitantly challenged each other, sometimes finally just agreeing to disagree, but always in a friendly

and respectful manner. They clearly enjoyed each other's company
and, when the dialogue ended, they resolved to meet again soon.

Censorship / De-Emphasis of Government Funding for the Arts

Nichols: Censorship seems to coming back. In other words we seem to be having a radical swing toward conservatism in the arts and everything in this country.

Anaya: What do you mean, "seem to be"? We are.

Nichols: Yes, we are. Well, I say "seem to be" because the fact is that underneath the liberal veneer our culture has been pretty conservative for years. In other words, Reagan is not all that different from Jimmy Carter except that Jimmy Carter had more of a liberal patina. That's my feeling. I feel that underneath—

Anaya: But I don't think the question here is one of Jimmy Carter or Reagan. I think the question here, as I understand it, is the state agencies having money to give writers and artists in the state for projects. And on the federal level the NEA, which is the biggest, and that came up last year— something like 50 percent cut in their budget. And a lot of people got together and wrote their congressmen and wrote letters.

I think the emphasis is kind of one of priority. If you're gonna talk about Reagan, he prizes a certain kind of Hollywood art. His buddies from Holly- wood—his background in that area. Whereas I would imagine the NEA as a governmental federal agency would be interested across the board—dance, theater.

Nichols: Sure, but everyone has been cut by the Reagan administration. Isn't NEA gonna have a lot less, and state agencies are gonna have a lot less bread. I used to sit on the panels in New Mexico when grants were given out and for years it was almost laughable what they had to give out in this state. It was so little money. I think it was a couple of grand—$2 or $3 thousand— and there'd be people fighting to get $600 or $500.

Anaya: Essentially, then, what you are saying is that there has never been an emphasis.

Nichols: Right, there has never been an emphasis, so how can you de- emphasize it. The arts during the time that I have worked with agencies that fund arts, specifically in the writing area,—it's always been difficult to get money for writers because nobody wants to fund a writer who is going to write what he wants. It is easy to get money to dance or opera, because they are noncontroversial. To give money to a writer, if he keeps his freedom to write what he wants—people get skittery. The thing that always bothered me is that most of the groups and organizations that give out money, say, to writers also often want to lay their bread on someone who has already kind of made it. I remember when I published my first novel and it was a Literary Guild alternate and being made into a movie and I was just raking in money hand over fist, I was approached by the Rockefeller Foundation. They came to me and asked me to apply for a grant and I told them, "Hey, man, I'm just rolling in dough, but I have three friends who I think are really fine writers who are dead broke. Give me the applications and I'll have them apply." They said, "Don't bother." In other words, they wanted to give money to somebody who was already a bona fide winner so that my popularity would give their foundation credit. And I find that attitude to be fairly prevalent in a lot of money that has been given to the arts, even though I don't have a lot of personal experience with that.

Anaya: It's true that it's almost like a cycle. You have to produce to apply, and as you produce you kind of open a lot of avenues for your own earnings.

Nichols: You can go look at half the novels of Bernard Malamud and Philip Roth and Saul Bellow and see that these best-selling books have a little blurb inside that says the writer wishes to thank the Guggenheim Foundation or the NEA for their liberal grants in helping me write this book. And I find that very disturbing, plus I think in the past it has always been extraordinarily difficult for either political people or minority people in this country to get grants, let alone get published. Rudy knows a lot more about that than I do—just the kind of censorship against working class or minority class people in this country getting into mainstream publishing. And I think that rolls over into the grants and government.

Moderator: We started out discussing censorship. We move to de-emphasis of the arts, and we never talked—

Nichols: Well, it's the same thing. When you de-emphasize government funding for the arts, that's a form of censorship. When a publisher doesn't publish certain kinds of material, that's censorship.

Anaya: Let me raise this question, John. Which we didn't even consider. Should the government be funding writers—the arts, I think is the first question.

Nichols: Yes, of course it should. The government has an obligation to all its populace—not just to fund its writers. It has an obligation to take care of old people. It has an obligation to provide medical care to farmers and growers, so why not writers and artists? The government goes around yanking people off of welfare at the same time that it gives Chrysler how many billions of dollars to bail them out. The rich get the welfare and the welfare recipients don't get nothing.

Anaya: Then the other real question is what happens once you accept government funding? Are your hands tied? Are there certain things you have to do? I know I received an NEA fellowship, and I was never told anything at all during the term of my fellowship, absolutely nothing. So that, I think, is a fellowship that we want to encourage and lobby for. On the other hand, like the question you asked earlier, I never received the funding when I was working on the first book when I really—

Nichols: When you needed it!

Anaya: How do we find the writers who are just beginning and who have a lot of talent, and they're really good, and push them into those funding agencies and encourage them to apply?

Nichols: I don't know how you do that, but I think that basically who they are and whether they have talent or not is fairly obvious, and they're just ignored. I know a lot of writers who publish maybe a few stories in small magazines, a novel that didn't go anywhere, but amongst writers and people in the cultural world, they're quite respected. There are a few of those people that actually learn how to play the politics to get a grant. But even the initial funding in a sense isn't enough, is it? It's just a start. But then anyway a start is often a start. You get some jumper cables and somebody gets your car started and you can go far, you know.

Anaya: But you have to buy the battery.

Nichols: Yeah, you gotta have a battery. Metaphors are fun. You can tell there's some literary heavyweights at work here. I don't know. I'm not real familiar with the infrastructure. Maybe Rudy knows a lot more, being a professor also involved with academia. He'd probably have a better pipeline into how its all functioning, than I do. As far as censorship is concerned, there's all kinds of censorship. There's obvious censorship, such as one of the more famous cases in New Mexico when *Bless Me, Ultima* was banned by the Bloomfield school board, which raised a lot of hackles and aroused a rallying

cry and has been symbolic of stuff. I remember I cut out of the paper about
a month ago a little article that the school board in Vermont, upstate Vermont,
was yanking all the Steinbeck out of their library.

Anaya: But in most of the things I'm reading now, it seems to me that
there's a rise in censorship. Every time I pick up an article or a news bulletin
on tv. I got a paper from New York yesterday. The *Jewish Women's National
Newspaper.* They are also very aware that there's a rise—I think because of
the time we live in—a rise in the moral majority and the righteous right, or
whatever they call themselves, and maybe that is part of what we were talking
about earlier, having to do with the political—what's happening in the political arena filters down, and these people see—reflect on it—and say, "Well,
now is our time to move." They feel that they're getting a stamp from the
man in power to pull off these things, to burn books, to pull them from
libraries and to ban films. I would say it's really bad today, from the reading
that I'm doing.

Nichols: And what gets published is a form of censorship. What becomes
just economical. What people will buy. What people will advertise becomes
a form of censorship. I know, for example, that one of the representative
booksellers that works for my publisher got really freaked out when they read
a report—I think it's the New Mexico Authors' League sent around to papers
last year or the year before—asking what were the three most influential
books in your life. I wrote back that I thought the three most influential
books—I think one of them was Emile Zola's *Germinale* and one of them
was Karl Marx's *Kapital,* and I explained why. This guy somehow came
across that answer—it was published somewhere—and told Holt that they
didn't want to sell a book that was written by a communist. And Holt got in
a real flap. I mean Holt told him to just go and fuck himself. But there's a lot
of that kind of tension when more recently in this book I just mentioned—I
got a book coming out next year—which has photographs in it and, again,
the marketing people at my publisher, after a conference with the representatives, asked me to take out three nude photographs in the book because they
felt that the kind of audience that would buy the book was the same audience
they figure that bought *If Mountains Die,* would be middle-class, fifty-year-
old Texas matrons, and if they saw a nude photograph in the book, they would
be really shocked and wouldn't buy the book. But it was also presented to
me that they felt that the publisher would print 20,000 copies without the
three nudes in the book and only 10,000 copies with the three nudes in the

book. And that's something that seems real archaic. We've gone through the *Ulysses,* D. H. Lawrence, William Burroughs type struggles far in the past, and yet those kind of struggles may be coming back.

Anaya: The censorship—well, there's all sorts of levels we haven't covered, like you mentioned earlier, John. Women and minorities in this country have, and are still being, excluded from publishing in big firms. That means you never get—it's very difficult to ever get a national reading public when you have to work with a small press. Someone at the writer's congress, in one of the addresses, talked about the censorship of slow-moving books. It's gotten to the point that if your book is moving very slowly, they shred it. That's a censorship. I think this moral majority and the religious right is really organized in this country, and what they're doing is they are putting an extreme amount of pressure on publishers, on textbook publishers. They're organized because they have mailing lists, money, computers to work with, and the writers find themselves very isolated. You're working in Albuquerque or in Taos and somebody burns your book or somebody tells you to cut out x amount of photographs or a chapter. You say, "Well, what can I do about this because they've got the leverage." And these people are putting out mail, and calling, and raising money. Imagine the tremendous pressure that they put on the publisher to cut books before they even get published. That's censorship, and that's what's happening now. That's the most frightening thing that's happened right now. We can live without a lot of money in publishing because writers traditionally have anyway, but at least to have the hope that your work would get published, and now it's being cut.

Nichols: I think that I just can't say enough about censorship but I don't want to stay just on that topic. In a certain sense there are little holes in the system—I think I sort of fit into one of the little holes in the system. Some of the work that I do is pretty heavy politically, and straight publishing has published my stuff. And for that I'm grateful—that I have been lucky to have a certain kind of national exposure. I also know that in a sense that's a kind of exception. But those little holes are there. I know that this isn't exactly writing, but in the history, for example, of having my novel *Milagro Beanfield War* on film option, trying to be made into a movie, there's an enormous amount of censorship that begins with the heads of just about every major studio that's either put up money for it or been approached. They'll just say, "Who wants to see a movie about a bunch of Mexicans?" The racism is so prevalent in that industry against doing a project which involves not middle-class white people, which involves either minority or working class people, and also a project which is about class struggle. Nobody in this country wants to either publish books or make movies about class struggle.

Public Reading Habits

Anaya: How about this "public reading habits as you perceive them." Do you perceive anything, or something, or you don't care?

Nichols: Well, I care a lot. Every writer cares about public reading habits. All the cliches are electronic and visual—and nobody's reading anymore.

Anaya: You can't write to the public.

Nichols: No, but—
Anaya: Well, why do you care?

Nichols: Wait a minute. Start again there.
Anaya: "Public reading habits as you perceive them." Why should you perceive them, I ask. Because if you perceive them, then you know what they're like and you write to them.

Nichols: I wouldn't say that I write to them, but I try to write—it's very important to me to reach the public. In other words, I would consciously try to develop a lot of lines—I'm talking about class lines and educational lines, rather than going the other way, like *Ulysses* and *Gravity's Rainbow*. That doesn't interest me.

Anaya: Yes, but let me ask you this. Your books are long. Does the public read long books?

Nichols: Sure. The public goes in. They don't care what's in it. They just buy it by the pound. Basically, people feel they're getting a better deal if they get a three-pound book for $14 than if they only get a one-pound book.

Anaya: Then that's what I'm going to start writing—the three-pound books.

Nichols: You've gotta write a three-pound book. There are more books published each year than have ever been published before in the history of the country. In other words, there are millions and millions of books that are coming out every year.

Anaya: Do you know where the role of fiction is in those books? It's diminishing.

Nichols: It is diminishing. However, since I got into the business, everybody has told me the novel is dead. And if you listen to people, you wouldn't do anything in life.

Anaya: Well, it holds for some writers more than for others.

Nichols: Of course, in other words the odds against you were more than the odds against me.

Anaya: It's not only you, it's the way the system is built. It rewards some and it doesn't reward others.

Nichols: Sure.

Anaya: I think it has a purpose, an intent. If you exclude minority writers from writing, you exclude their voice in American literature.

Nichols: You also exclude their voices of power in the economic structure of the country, which is even more important.

Anaya: Well, actually I don't think they give a damn about the economic power.

Nichols: Yes, they do. I think it's very much—

Anaya: Well, if you don't have economic power, why would they care?

Nichols: Because your role as a person without economic power is very important in an economic structure which depends on people with no power to do the shit labor that the corporations and businesses make their profits off of. That's real important to understand to me.

Anaya: Yes, that's important, but it's also important to understand on a—I would say economics is important but what also is important on a gut level is the culture itself.

Nichols: Right.

Anaya: If you exclude people from talking about the values of their culture and using it as a background in the arts, then you extinguish that culture and you put it to the side as a kind of quaint prop where you can go fill yourself up once a year with tacos and beans. You don't have to really see or care about these people.

Nichols: The important thing about it is you keep people in their class. You keep people in a working class position with whose labor profits can be made in the country. That's the most important thing about denying people their culture. You deny them the power to get out of the working-class or a

subjugated or exploited position. And you've got to have, in a country like
ours, 60 million or 80 million people in an exploited position for the economy
to function, and part of maintaining people in that position is to deny them
their culture. It's a tool to keep them there.

Anaya: That's where I'm coming from because I think even as much as
Chicano writers in this country have published today, you still haven't
changed the economic and social well-being of the people. The people who
are changing that are wheeling and dealing on other levels, in other arenas.

Nichols: But as long as they are doing it with capitalist guidelines and
rules they're never going to change the situation in the country.

Anaya: Of course they are. Why not?

Nichols: How can they? They can't.

Anaya: For example, if you have somebody that can use the system and
creates room for more Chicano professionals and people that are educated. I
think that's positive.

Nichols: That's positive up to a point, but what happens if people are
allowed to partake of the system doing exactly what everybody else is
doing—for example, if women are allowed to rise in the corporate structure,
to get salaries equal with men—that's good, except that they're still going to
have to step all over other women or other men to get there, because that's
the way the system runs. If you don't change the system, every time a woman
rises, a man will fall.

Anaya: All systems run like that.

Nichols: No, they don't.

Anaya: Which one doesn't?

Nichols: What do you mean, which one doesn't?

Anaya: Give us an example.

Nichols: Okay. Every system has lots of flaws, as far as I'm concerned.
But I feel that it's important you have a blueprint or an ideology, things that
you believe in. For me, it's understanding economics from a Marxist perspective. I would like to see a society where the distribution of wealth is equal,
because I think it's unfair for me to be able to earn a hundred thousand
dollars a year writing for movies, while an undocumented worker from Mexico gets paid $2 an hour and is shit on for putting the food on my table. That

is not the way to run the world, and as long as we live in a capitalist society that's the way it's going to function.

Anaya: How do you change it? Why is it right for you to take the talent that you have and make a living?

Nichols: There's nothing wrong with that, no.

Anaya: If you get too much money, give it to somebody else.

Nichols: I do. I do. You make a living too. But what's wrong is that for me to make a hundred thousand dollars, there has to be 150–200 workers in the Mesilla Valley who are earning slave wages. Whose kids can't go to school.

Anaya: Go organize them.

Nichols: I'll work on that. I think my books and my literature—

Anaya: Your talent is to write.

Nichols: Okay, but my writing—it's important for me in my writing to speak of those problems. Writing is very important in organizing. It's very important in working on creating people's consciousness about—

Anaya: Let me ask you about that. How many people of those workers in the Mesilla Valley got organized when they read your book?

Nichols: My book and lots of other people's books and people's films are important in creating the consciousness of various people who are involved at all levels of trying to change the society.

Anaya: But you have to have people to go down—

Nichols: But the people who go down—creating people who are concerned with it; one of the things that gets people concerned is your book, my book, other people's books. One of the reasons I've changed my—I've done a lot of organizing in my life. I still do it. But mostly I think the writing is more important because I reach more people and add to the kind of ambience that, first of all, makes people feel hopeful it can be done, which is very important. If people are cynical, if they see no hope, they're not even going to be interested in organizing.

Anaya: Well, I could say that that's—that you're rationalizing that you reach more people. You're saying, "I want to keep writing, so I really reach more people by writing," and I say, "That guy's rationalizing." Why don't you really go down and work with—at a plant or with farmworkers, if that's really where you think the movement should come? And the same holds true for myself.

Nichols: But the movement is not made up of just doing one thing. The movement is made up of hundreds of particles that go together. Books are one of the important particles. Music is another important particle. Teaching is another important particle. Legal aid lawyers are another important particle. I get lots of letters from people who say that my books make them feel guilty or make them feel good about organizing or stuff like that. That's nice. That's my little addition.

Anaya: Right. Your talent is writing.

Nichols: Right. But it's important to be connected, to—what's interesting to me is that until I was about thirty-three I never considered myself a writer because I was torn between being on the barricades and writing, and I spent half my life on the barricades and couldn't do it really well because I always wanted to go home and write. And when I was at home writing, I felt real guilty for not being on the barricades. But when I was thirty-two when I sat down to write *Milagro*—when I was thirty-three I guess—I finally said, "Nichols, for better or for worse, this is what you seem to want to do and can do the best, so why don't you get down to business and try and really learn how to do it."

Fiction is very political—90 percent of the novels. I just read a novel called *A Flag for Sunrise*, Robert Stone, have you heard of that book? Robert Stone wrote *Hall of Mirrors, Dog Soldiers*—he's a best selling author. He's nominated for the National Book Award. It's a cynical, vicious, nasty, cruel, ugly book, which just has no hope for anybody. There's no idealism, no nothing in it. It's just—it's one of the most despair-laden and nasty things I've ever read. It's the most highly praised book of the year in this country, and you get that again and again. That's very political. That's the kind of book that gets lauded and touted in our society. That kind of cynicism, I think, again getting back to economics, really functions. If people are really cynical and feel there's no point in getting involved, why try and change the world, why work for something better? Then they can justify just saying "I'm going to look out for number one; I'm going to learn about power, how to get it, how to use it. I believe in the virtue of selfishness." And you don't care about anything else. Books like that are very political because they create the attitudes of a whole culture, and they're horrible attitudes. They are antithetical against the hope and love of a book like *Bless Me, Ultima* or you can think of—or what's the book? *Sangre* [by Leroy Quintana]—Did you read that? This gentle, compassionate—that has feelings of hope and caring and stuff like that. So much of our literature and fiction creates just real hard-nosed, nasty cynical attitudes which allow people to justify just looking after themselves—eat, drink, and be merry, for tomorrow we're all gonna die. So nobody cares or has a commitment for anything beyond themselves.

Anaya: I just don't see too many of the migrant trucks as they're coming up and back and forth, nobody's reading novels. So I mean are we in the wrong business? What should we be writing? If you know what it would take to change the system—

Nichols: No, I think that's a wrong statement. First, I lived in Albuquerque when *Bless Me, Ultima* started to become real popular. And you would not believe the range of people that told me they read that book and liked it.

Anaya: We're getting back to the presentation of a world view and a cultural background that people identify with. That's more where I come from in presentation of that, so to speak, as opposed to an up-front political statement.

Nichols: But that's political.

Anaya: Of course, that's political, but that's the question I'm asking. How do we get the books to the workers on the trucks, traveling back and forth in the migrant stream? How do we get them there?

Nichols: You interest them. My guess is that you've had a lot of people who were in that stream or around it who told you they've read your book. I've had a lot of people who were in that stream or around it who told me they've read my book.

In this country the thing that's really incredible is that if you go outside the borders of the United States, the poets and the writers are much more important to the working class of that country. The problem is all my relatives in France think that Americans are Phillistines because basically most Americans aren't interested in culture.

Anaya: I think that may be a myth.

Nichols: It's not a myth.

Anaya: I think so. Given your own philosophy that you say you espouse, you know very often that the working class—and it doesn't matter in which, in most countries in the world—is isolated. It doesn't have the time and it doesn't have the economic needs to get that involved.

Nichols: No, that's not true. In Latin America the working class is so much more involved in awareness of literature and in the working literature. In Europe the working class is much more involved.

Anaya: I go a lot to Mexico—

Nichols: In Italy—

Anaya: Wait a minute! Wait a minute! I want to give you an example.

Nichols: I go to the latest opera or whatever—I'm not into opera—I think opera is for real cone-heads, but in Italy and Austria and France and Germany, opera is something people dig.

Anaya: I travel in Mexico. On the one hand, I would have to say I agree with you. I see the workers, people going back and forth, they're reading magazines, they're reading novels. They're very active. But then you get to another level of workers, and they don't have anything. And that's where I'm saying there's a myth. We can say that that is happening, but it's not happening here. The working class in this country has turned not to artists like yourself—not to writers—they have turned to the media. The key is in television—cable television. The poorest family will put their assets into getting cable in instead of buying a novel. So you got to deal with that reality.

(interlude)

Nichols: I know. I know. But I want to say one thing. I want to say one thing. I need to say something real important here. First of all, the United States of America is the most isolated country in the world.

Anaya: That's nonsense! That's nonsense!

(Anaya and Nichols speaking simultaneously)

Nichols: That media component don't tell us nothing about two thirds of the rest of the world.

Anaya: It's trying not to tell you anything—

Nichols: All right, all right—let me finish what I'm saying then. The United States of America has the least historical perspective of any country in the world. We have absolutely no concept—

Anaya: No . . . but when you say this country—

Nichols: I'm talking about the USA.

Anaya: I know, but you say "we." I can't identify with that. I don't know what you're talking about. Who is "we"?

Nichols: What I'm talking about—

Anaya: Well, you know, Chicanos in the Southwest are forced into the U.S. system.

Nichols: I got caught up in the same damn system—

Anaya: But how can you say "we"? How can you say "we"? What do you mean—"we"?

Nichols: I mean "we"—I mean—

Anaya: I can't identify with that. Up to now, it means workers that you're talking about. They can't identify with that.

Nichols: They can identify with it because they live in this country. Because they live under the laws of this country. They get this country's newspapers. They are forced into this country's educational system whether they like it or not. They are programmed into—

Anaya: I don't believe that programming's right. I don't believe you should use a word like that because—

Nichols: Did I say "program"?

Anaya: We're not programmed. If you look at—if you study the cultures that are surviving in this country right now, what you will find, I think, is that they have a value system so deep and ingrained in them from the past that they're not buying into the program, John. That's what interesting about it. They're not buying into it. What scares me the most is the television media, because that's what's programming minds, and that's what's spreading the great American myth, the great American value system. But the minute you say that, I say to myself "I wonder what he's talking about?" because that really should not be a part of my world. It's a capitalist value system.

Nichols: Well, we live in a capitalist system. The cultures that are surviving—not just black culture, or Cherokee culture, Chicano culture—there's also Slavic and Yugoslavian and Czechoslovakian. New York City has forty or fifty foreign language newspapers, and every other block has a different culture that's theoretically surviving; however, everybody is under the gun of an economic system which pretty much calls the shots. You turn on your tv and you're brainwashed—what, 40 percent of every show is brainwashing you into the capitalist system. You pick up the *New York Times* magazine, probably 60 percent of it print—and this magazine is brainwashing you to think a certain way. If you've got a dishwasher or a central heating system or whatever, real estate problems, you're being brainwashed to think a certain way. All of us are in it. I'm in it. You're in it. We're all in it. We all deal with it. That's what I mean when I say "we" I don't see any culture, from the Taos Pueblo to white farmers in upstate Vermont, who are surviving it any better. All of them.

Anaya: Right, I was just going to ask—

Nichols: The point is—when I say "we" I am talking about an American system which systematically programs us all to feel a certain way about the cars we drive, the schools we're in. It programs attitudes, and it also keep us ignorant of what's happening in the rest of the world. All of us are programmed.

Anaya: Well, everybody agrees with that.

Nichols: Okay, good. But the point is to fight against that because it is so, not only counterproductive, but it is eviscerating—the vitality.

Anaya: You have to give people credit. They're already doing that. I know what I watch on tv, and I watch the news and I know what percentage of that is slush. And I don't buy the *New York Times.* So I'm not buying all of that. And I have this sense that people I know, in my community, know what they are buying. I think the point is to make people more aware so that they are educated so that when they make choices that are very clear to them, and let them know where they are going. It's not so much to get down on the system and knock it around—because it's so big. I don't know what it means when you start railing against it, but you take your own community and you work with it, and say, "Here's what we're all about. Here's what our history is like. Here's what our values are like. Now, where do we want to go from here, folks?" Not just to tell them it's bad for them—let them decide. Who are we to tell them? Somebody is always telling us how to be in order to fight back or to try and be the way you want them to be. I mean, you have to fight back actively. You can't just be passive.

Nichols: I agree.

The Novel

Nichols: The novel, I think, is a form that chooses you as much as you choose it. It gives you a lot of space to work out characters and interactions, and since I couldn't be a poet, I found out very early in life that I didn't have—I didn't have that gift for the really concise—the whole thing—put on one page. I wandered into the long story. "I wandered lonely as a cloud . . ."

Anaya: And there I spied a novel . . .

Nichols: I think there's a kind of precedent for it in my background. I come from a family of story-tellers, and not just a family of current story-tellers, but everybody in my family begins their stories with "Well, in 1864 or in 1653, when we came over on the *Mayflower* (laughter), great-great-great-granddaddy so-and-so. . . ." And in a place like Taos people talk like that. Even a simple statement in a meeting—somebody would get up and say—the purpose would be they were going to give the reason why they were gonna donate $10 to the Tres Rios Association—but they'd spend half an hour doing it. I grew up where just telling these stories was important. New Mexico is a place where people are story-tellers. This country is a place where people are story-tellers, but it's been suppressed in a lot of areas. My feeling about the novel—and this may just be pure out-and-out ego and chauvinistic, jingoistic rhetoric—is that the novel is the kind of medium where you can do more than any other medium. It's just open, so ample, so wide. The most ample medium that exists is the novel. You can literally deal more with the whole, wide panorama. If you're interested in a macroscopic overview of life, society, personality, social interaction, the novel seems to be the best medium. I don't think that's just arrogant. I really think that you can address more questions—

Anaya: I think that's an old middle-class view. For one thing, we keep—I keep trying to draw us back to the power that the media—television and movies—have, which are taking over the precise definition that you've just given, in a very real sense. No, they don't do it, but I just wonder if we shouldn't be writing soap operas and telenovellas, because that's all the people that stay home and working people—a great deal of what they're seeing and viewing and listening to is that. So we might be outdated in a sense in defining the novel in that way.

Nichols: You're right. You're very right, and if we live within a system which would produce teledramas that have some kind of feeling or real conscience, then we'd be in that.

Anaya: I agree, but isn't our responsibility—for example, yours since you are starting to use your writing for movies—I have this project—I'm also writing a tv play. [We want] to get into that media as once we tried to get into the media of publication.

Nichols: Yes, you're right, and I suppose I work in the movies partially for that reason, partially because if a movie is made of your book, the book—if there is a movie—will stay in print for the next ten years, and that many more people will read the book, and they'll go to the movies and then read the book.

Anaya: I'm not knocking reading, because I think that's where America, in terms of involvement with an art, an art form—

Nichols: Language just to promote and to continue the language is special, because films don't do it and television.

Anaya: I think they can though. They can. It's there. They could.

Nichols: The question is politically forcing them to do it.

Anaya: Let me ask you this question. I once had a friend, a novelist, who said he went to the seashore—it was on Sunday—and he said, "I walked the entire length of the beach, and there were all these people on the beach and they were all sunning and they were all reading a book." He said, "Not a single person was reading any one of the books we're writing—as serious writers."

Nichols: Serious writing, in a sense, has never been lauded from the dawn of time. I think of little examples like Herman Melville sold twenty copies of *Moby Dick* before he died, that's all.

Anaya: But the point is when we downplay the soap opera or the telenovella and we say that is not preserving or teaching the language or what we want put up front, who are we deluding? Do people really want to listen to us?

Nichols: Yes. You know why? Because in Shakespeare's time and Cervantes' time there were hundreds of telenovellas and soap opera writers who disappeared because what they wrote was irrelevant. Cervantes survived; Shakespeare survived because in essence, things get weeded out. History weeds out what's relevant and what's irrelevant.

Anaya: Yes, but history is the very people you were talking about awhile ago—those in power.

Nichols: But the point of fact is—

Anaya: Academics weed out. Do you want them to weed out your work?

Nichols: No. In a sense, there's a hope that there's a process of weeding out that's above and beyond the politicians, the academics, and everyone—something that's good survives—

Anaya: The change is so drastic in the public—to answer one of those questions—the public reading and viewing habit is so strong that all that survives is the soap operas.

Nichols: They won't. It's almost as if—
Anaya: I don't agree—and I don't want to agree—I'm just raising the question.

Nichols: Okay, if you trust in history, they won't. In other words, for some reason there's a process in history that weeds out—you know, the popular song of this year is gone next year.
Anaya: But history is controlled.

Nichols: No. History is no more controlled than photosynthesis. In other words, history—people think they can control history against its natural rhythm, but they can't. I don't know if that's clear—

Contemporary Fiction

Nichols: Well, that's heavy. It's almost like—the novel, why have you chosen this form? It's like the alcoholic—why do you choose scotch instead of bourbon? Or beer instead of Gallo. Contemporary fiction you respect most, okay. For me, in twenty-five words or less, I respect a fiction that has compassion and that has hope, that chooses to take responsibility for some kind of social conscience, doesn't have to be overtly political, but it just has a commitment toward adding positively to culture, period.
Anaya: I think that's a good starting point. I also like writers who push themselves and experiment with language and form. I don't like fiction that is set in a formula or a type—detective stories and cowboy stories and stories in that genre bore me because you can often predict what's going to happen in the plot and the characters aren't strong enough to take over and to really make the story intriguing. I like the contemporary writers that can not only tell the story on one level, but can also experiment so much with the form itself, with the language and what's happening in it, that they challenge me. I think the sense of compassion that John spoke about—the human compassion—and addressing human problems in a positive way—

Nichols: I hate the cynical, nihilistic stuff. I'll read a lot of—
Anaya: I think there can be a lot positive in writing about people who seem almost doomed by their circumstances. By that I mean that sometimes

people—or the characters you use to represent some of those people out there—are so strong. There can be a cynical character or there can be a downbeat character who, because of what he is or what she is, becomes kind of like a strength-maker within the work itself, a person of power.

Nichols: Yes. I mentioned this book by Robert Stone, whom I think is a very good writer, and yet I'm just appalled at the nihilism in his vision. I think that guys like Thomas McGuane are real gifted writers, and yet I have no sympathy for their vision. I'll read somebody like Joan Didion in a book like *Play It As It Lays,* and I can learn a lot about real clear, lucid writing, and yet I have absolutely no sympathy for that vision. Jerzy Kosinski in his first book, *The Painted Bird,* moved me a lot, because it's about despair and expresses that vision in a way that articulates that vision in a positive kind of light. And yet everything that came since—the four books afterward that I read—I just got pissed off. I said, "This is just sort of exploitive ugliness."

Anaya: It might be that the function of the story-teller in contemporary society is to try to hold on to that positive vision of the world and what it can be.

Nichols: Yes, I think writers, in a sense, are sort of the new priests. I would much rather—I relate much more to Leslie Silko doing *Ceremony* or to Scott Momaday doing *House Made of Dawn* or something like that. To me, it's just important to have a certain kind of care and an enormous amount of hope involved, even if you're talking about the state of despair. But that has hope involved rather than just "that's the way it is—tough beans—too bad" type shit, which is what the majority of successful stuff—is. I haven't read a whole lot of southwestern writing or something, but I really like things like Leroy Quintana's *Sangre* and things like that. It's almost like daring to care on levels that the mass media say is not sophisticated. I really despise cynicism, and I believe that underlying a vision—things that I relate to—need to have hope, which is why my latest book [*Nirvana Blues*] makes me a little nervous. It's about people who don't have hope. It's written from inside a bourgeois head, and I worry a lot that it's not clear where I'm at, because I've chosen to take a position. It's written about people who don't have hope. Eighty percent of the people I know don't have hope. It's sad. And they have lots of money, and they have wonderful houses, and they're so involved in themselves. They've got hot tubs and gurus. But they're miserable because they get no fulfillment.

Anaya: Who are all these people you are running around with?

Nichols: Middle-class America. I don't run around a whole lot, but you—you live a certain part of your life in academia and you must have a lot of insights into the problems and the good things and the bad things there—the lifestyles of people who in a sense have it made and yet who are very unhappy, who don't find fulfillment.

Anaya: Academia is like the working class.

Nichols: Partially. My dad's in academia and his stories—it's scary.

Anaya: But I think most of the people that are really—they may not consider themselves the working class or see themselves as workers. And I think that's the way we see ourselves, and a big percentage of the department I work in are people really interested in scholarship or literature or teaching.

Nichols: But the role of academia is basically to teach and to be hopeful. Why do you teach? It's because you have hope. Because you believe people can learn and progress, and that knowledge has a value—spiritual. One of the problems with academia is that so much of it is translated into "What can I learn in order to earn a living" rather than "What can I learn just—" I got 80 percent of my values and sensibilities from teachers, from people who were good and even if I didn't realize it at the moment, they introduced me to things that when I got out of school and then when I really came to where I wanted to learn, they had taught me where to look.

Anaya: You make me feel like going back to teaching now.

Perspectives: Early Work and Most Recent Work

Nichols: Between my second and third novel there was a nine-year hiatus during which I completely re-learned sociology, history.

Anaya: What did you write that got made into a movie?

Nichols: *The Sterile Cuckoo?* It's a neat little book. It's so funny, just a love affair between a boy and a girl. That's the difference between my early and later work. It's just basically a total redefinition of why I'm alive, what my sensibilities are, what my politics are, what I understand the world to be, and what I'm striving for. This blew out the foundations of what I thought I was going to be, and made my life a lot harder.

Anaya: I think every work whether it's a novel or a short story is a learning process. Almost every single one. I have to learn to read, to write, all over again. I think the differences are, for me, in kind of recording what I wanted to record in terms of steps. The first three novels—I've learned a whole hell of a lot. The tragedy in my life is that I used to think that someday in my life I would become a professional and have a lot of confidence about going forward. And I have less confidence now, in a sense, than I did twenty years ago.

I would say that from my early work what I have done in every work I've ever done is challenge myself, to grow, to tackle new things, new ideas, and I don't want to repeat myself.

Nichols: I've found that basically the way I used to feel is that every work had to be a major qualitative step forward; then I realized that every time out of the barn you can't do that. *The Magic Journey* for me—I poured everything into that. That means more to me than anything I ever did, and yet after it, I didn't want to just repeat myself, say the same shit. And it takes you awhile to move on—

Anaya: But all of your three novels are dealing with the Taos area.

Nichols: They're set in sort of a northern New Mexico setting, but as far as I'm concerned they have as much to say about New York City as they do about anyplace else. On other levels it's just—I keep telling people that the same system operates in Taos, New Mexico, that operates in Chicago or Los Angeles or New York. Not only that but everybody in Taos watches the same tv shows, reads the same national magazines with the same advertising, goes to a school system which is controlled nationwide so that the education the kid is getting in Taos is the same education they're getting in Montpelier, Vermont, or Nashville, Tennessee. It really is. That's what's important. You take a book like *The Magic Journey* which is about how capitalism works, and it's about the genocide of a people in the process. You go to any town in America and that's the history of that town.

Anaya: In *Nirvana Blues*—this guy—you say he was searching for dope that was supposed to come in? Are you saying that all over the country all of these people are going through that?

Nichols: No, all over the country everybody is making that score. In the United States everybody is into making the fast score, the big score, to get your security, to do this, do that, go to Colombia, get emeralds, get diamonds. Do something to make the big score. Get your security, buy your place. Get it made. It just seemed like a universal situation to me. Most people are totally confused. You're not confused, but most people are thoroughly confused. They're confused because in a sense—I'm talking about middle-class America, which is mostly white America, which is what that book's about—they're confused because everything they've been taught to think they ought to get in order to be satisfied they have received and instead of getting fulfillment out of it, they're desperate. Eighty grand a year doesn't get you nothing. Your house and three acres of land doesn't get you nothing. . . .

Moderator: Okay, goals.
Anaya: I would like to live to be a hundred and have an active life.

Nichols: With a capital L, right?
Anaya: Other than that, nothing else interests me.

Nichols: Goals. My goals are all connected with work. Right now my basic goal is to write a long novel epic. About the rise of industrial capitalism in the United States from after the Civil War until the present day.

Moderator: Could both of you talk about your goals in your fiction, specifically? Not just about current projects.

Nichols: Well, it's hard to talk about the future. I just deal with what I'm writing right now. I'm trying to get a teleplay done for CPB.

Moderator: What is CPB?

Nichols: Corporation for Public Broadcasting. And over the last ten years I've been writing short stories and I'm working on revising and editing them.

(Inaudible discussion of sequence of questions.)

Nichols: My first major goal is simply to add positively to our culture—and I think it's important to care about adding positively. The second goal is to be part of, to be a little molecule in the cultural part of the revolutionary movement which will one day terminate the capitalist control of the people and the economy and the culture, . . . humbly speaking. (Laughter) I'm real serious. One of the things that gives my life a whole lot of meaning is that particularly since often if you're just dealing with your own local scene, or the U.S. scene, or the Southwest scene, there's a lot of defeat involved. But the thing that gives my life meaning is feeling connected at a much wider level to the revolutionary movement. So I'm not just talking about El Salvador or Yugoslavia or whatever. I'm talking about attempts to elevate the North American culture above the incredibly mundane and exploitive levels that the national media and national government and national economics dictate, which is—

Anaya: So you're pontificating—(Laughter)

Nichols: (Laughter) I'm one of the few people I know that has a real positive attitude about history, that isn't flabbergasted or dismayed over the nihilistic strains of our culture, or just the world at large. And part of that is that my particular vision of history seems hopeful to me, and I work with people who I hope are struggling—because they have hope—and that's incredible. I feel real lucky to be involved and to feel that way because I live in a town where 90 percent of the people are just full of despair. They have no concept of history. They don't work with people who see hope for the future. They just work with people who say, "Holy Fuck, we're gonna have a nuclear war, or the planet's gonna disintegrate, or pollution's gonna wipe us out, or we live in a country that's so goddamn racist that there's no hope of ever overcoming it." And that's real sad.

Anaya: Well, what importance is the place, the Southwest, to you, John?

Nichols: Oh.

Anaya: You said you were trying to write the universal literature. So you could be anywhere.

Nichols: It happens to be that the little town I live in has been an enormously rich and open, wonderful town. It's real important to me in that I hate homogeneous areas. I don't like living in just a middle-class area, an all-white area, or an all-black area, or whatever. It's real important to have a mixture of cultures and classes. Taos is like that. I keep repeating this—one of the questions that people would often ask me and I keep trying to defeat this—is people come up to me and say, "How could you know so much about our culture?"—this is often Spanish-speaking Chicano people—"if you only lived here for two and a half years?" There's other Chicano that say, "Nichols don't know nothing, or he's full of shit, or he don't know nothing about Chicano culture." That's irrelevant to me, but they'll come up to me and say, "How can you know so much about Chicano culture to write *Milagro Beanfield War* when you only lived here two years?" I reply that about 85–90 percent of what's in that book I knew before I ever got to Taos. It's universal. Each of us has distinguishing facial features that separates us a little bit. But basically it's a universal human struggle which is why I resent being classified as a regional writer, and I think you should too. Because

what you talk about—la llorona—it's universal. Those same myths and stuff
exist. Appalachia has will-o'-the-wisps, and jack o'lanterns that run through
the swamps making weird noises like la llorona makes in Taos. German business people in Nayak, New York, go to stations of the cross in three-piece
suits, just like the penitentes in La Puente or Los Ojos on Good Friday.
Therefore, when I think of place, I admit I love where I live. I live in an area
that still has a tradition in that. It's not just Chicano. It's like anybody who's
ever been connected with the earth—whether they're white or red or brown
or stuff like that. I really think of myself as an American writer. If I have an
ego problem, it's like I'd like people to think of me as an American writer,
not a Southwestern writer or a Taos writer, but as an American writer. For
me, the community I live in is a microcosm of the United States of America.
Another thing I tell people is that I learn more about New York City by living
in Taos than I ever did living in New York because when I lived in new York
it was so overwhelming that it just beat me down. When I got to Taos, it's
like everything that I ever encountered in New York became very clear because it was at a smaller level that was comprehensible. But it was the same
society, the same system. Everybody watched the same tv programs, pretty
much reacted to the same things a lot. New Mexico—I just love it. Where I
live. I don't like Albuquerque, but I love northern New Mexico. There's
something real intrinsic that I feel about New Mexico.

   Anaya: I would say that place might be more important than anything else
if you consider the fact that mythology can arise from place; that there are
places on the earth where the gods are more active and the mountains, or the
bluff or the palisades of rocks, actually become the voice that speaks to us
and which we interpret. I'm not sure that I've found that in American literature—I mean in the Eastern Seaboard American literature, unless of course
you take some of the works of cultural conflict, like the Civil War, which is
very important. But here, I think, if you look at the indigenous population
and if you look at the grid on the map, you begin to get a sense for the role
that the Rocky Mountains play on the north-south migration pattern and a
role that the earth in its features itself plays in conveying to man the voice of
the gods. I think man internalizes that and then uses them as his religious and
communal and spiritual sensibilities and rituals.

   The other thing—I have a bit of a disagreement with John when he says
this is like any other place because of all these things that have to do with
people and culture take place in other places. I think that that's true on the
surface, but I think that what interests me the most is to look beneath the

surface and that is to really come up with a vision of what a particular people are like. What is their value system, which would be a philosophical system? I just don't think you can equate what has happened in the Southwest and the indigenous peoples of the Southwest with Appalachia or New York. I think there's a very real difference; that the foundation of a world view came to rest here and was passed, of course through migration, into Meso-America and Latin America. These are fantastic cultures that have the archetypal pattern that would tie them in with all the peoples of the world, but the way in which they devolve their symbols and their language and their relationships with the cosmos is what's unique. We not only have the land which speaks to us, but we have a tremendous kind of vision of the world which the indigenous people have right here and have cultivated for centuries and centuries. This to me makes it—it's got to be different. It can't be the New England states that had a culture imposed on them during the past three or four hundred years.

Nichols: Wait a minute! The Southwest is nothing but having cultures imposed on them, from Cortés to Coronado to various Indian tribes before that. Everyone has had things imposed on them.

Anaya: That's not what I'm talking about. What I'm talking about is— goes further back into history. It's deeper. It's longer.

Nichols: Even the Native American tribes who came here came from elsewhere. I would only say—

Anaya: But they had the time to sit down, i.e., to evolve their communal life and to really think through their relationships, what it is they value and what it is they want to keep alive in ceremonies and rituals and religion. Whereas if we deal with the surface, we're talking about this constant imposition and movement and change.

Nichols: But every culture . . . comes out of hundreds of thousands of years—it's just like the culture out here does too now. My feeling is that one of the things that's real precious about the Southwest is that it's one of the last areas of the country to be invaded by the all-encompassing economic system attempting to deculture the people and bring them all into sameness.

Anaya: Everybody has a romantic view of the Southwest.

Nichols: The point is that the Southwest is not a more rich cultural area.

Anaya: Awhile ago you were saying that the most prevalent culture is the capitalist.

Nichols: That's not a culture. There's a difference between culture and economic system.

Anaya: Hasn't this imposed itself upon culture?

Nichols: Of course, it has. But it has imposed itself as much on Chicano culture as it has on French Canadian culture as it has on Czechoslovakian culture, as it has on two hundred years of white—

Anaya: But isn't that economic system eventually changing culture?

Nichols: It does. It tries to eradicate culture.

Anaya: Where has it changed it more in this country? You're saying it's equal everywhere.

Nichols: No. The Southwest in a sense is the last area of the country to be invaded. For that reason, probably the native cultures are stronger here still. In other words, the capitalist culture has made less inroads because it hasn't been working for 200 years. That's two hundred and fifty years of oppression that the Navajo or Apache haven't had, or even a city like Taos hasn't had. Taos basically—the pueblo enclaves in the Southwest were fairly coherent for 2-, 3-, 4-, 500 years, until the Spanish came and started eradicating people. There's about 300 years of a kind of mestizo mix.

Anaya: If you're only looking at the economic level or the economic influence and problems it creates, it seems to me you're only looking at one surface of the reality. Isn't there something beneath the place? We're talking about Southwest. And I'm saying there were cultures here long before the Españoles came, long before the Anglo American came.

Criticism / National Reputation: The Effects

Nichols: Just say "none" and we can go on. You become so inured to it that it's irrelevant. The last time—wait a minute, I don't knock criticism. Criticism is important, in creating an atmosphere whereby your work gets disseminated, so I don't knock it. I think critics are important to a writer just like agents or publishers are. I think that's important to say because we get really arrogant about criticism, nasty.

Anaya: We gotta be hopeful.

Nichols: I'm very careful. I treat an incredibly laudatory review in the same way that I treat an incredibly derogatory review. The hysteria is kind of equal on both sides. As far as affecting the work, it doesn't affect the work at all. But it's real nice to occasionally have critics that take your work seriously and do serious pieces on your work for people to read. That's very important, and it's very rewarding. Even if you might not agree with their vision, their vision is real important to people's understanding or just considering your work legitimate or worthwhile. I wouldn't put down critics at all. I'm not sure that either of us is what you would call nationally known.

Anaya: I think the interesting thing about having people all over the country or books being read in a few classes here or there is that, one, you get to meet those people, communicate with them. Very often you get invited to read and discuss your work in different places, and I think that that's invigorating for the self, but not necessarily for the work, unless, way down the line someplace you have been or a community you have seen works its way into an interesting part of a novel you might be working on. What I enjoy more about people knowing my work is just being able to get out and visit places and see people. And they're excited about literature. They're excited about what's happening and they want to—they let you know.

Nichols: That's neat. The greatest reward is just to realize that you've touched other people on an intimate level, in their lives.

Anaya: Yes. They'll come up to you and they'll tell you the strangest thing that they've picked out of a novel or a character or a question, and when you break it down, you say, "This is really interesting because it's affected them." It may be off the wall or from left field, but you say, "That's what they got." And the point is that the communication was made. But it has the immediate effect, for me, of inspiring me. Like any time I do a reading or do a lecture or take a trip, I come back hyped up. I say, "I'd better get going on my next work."

Nichols: My work, just getting it out there—has got me in touch with just very special people in my life.

Anaya: Is that a fringe benefit?

Nichols: Sure, but that's—I'm working—I just did a picture with Costa Gavras [*Missing*], the director of *Z* and *State of Siege*. I'm doing another with him.

Anaya: You mean you were an actor or what?

Nichols: The reason he got in touch with me was because of my work, and it has turned out to be one of the neatest relationships personally. It's like meeting a blood brother.

Anaya: The thing that interests me is that in terms of national recognition when you read a review or an article on a national level, what I'm saying is that doesn't interest me or please me as much as when students or people off the street that have come into a lecture or reading, and they come up at the end and they say, "Hey, I read your novel and it's what I like." And you get to talking with them. That to me is the key. That's what I like. That's what I enjoy. And I have a lot of articles that have been written on my work and they're interesting and they're challenging and it's the critic imposing his vision, to use John's words, on the work. That's rewarding, but I think the real reward comes from the people, people you don't know and wouldn't guess are interested in literature. Suddenly they ask you questions.

Nichols: Yes, I just did what you call a book tour, which I thought would just be a cynical, asshole experience, and it turned out to be really lovely. Part of it was that the people who are interested in having me sign books were running little political bookstores in funny towns, and I would just meet—90 percent of the people I met just moved me deeply. They were sort of serious and awkward, but they were real people—they were neat. And they're the people who have influenced my life and who are real important people. The connections you can make by sending this silly little tome out there are just very special. It opens doors. It's like magic. It's like a looking glass.

An Interview with Rudolfo A. Anaya

César A. González-T / 1985

From *Imagine: Chicano Poetry Journal*, 2.2 (Winter 1985): 1–9. Reprinted by permission of César A. González-T.

On the occasion of Rudolfo Anaya's visit to San Diego, California (March 29–31, 1985), to participate in the 5th Annual Xochicuicatl "Flor y Canto," poetry readings by the community, al aire libre, at Chicano Park under the Coronado Bridge. Organized by León Aztleca. The program included the following: Aztec ceremony for Mother Earth, offering of flowers, Aztec prayer for the spring equinox, words by Rudolfo Anaya, poetry recital, and health ceremony.

Some Questions—Atinadas y Desafinadas

César González: First of all, Rudy, would you please recount the story you told me yesterday of the gift of the turquoise that you are wearing and about Cruz at Taos Pueblo. You mentioned three dreams in your forthcoming China journal, with their verisimilitudes in experience when you returned home. You spoke of your grandfather and Cruz as guides.

Rudolfo Anaya: In the summer of 1984, May and June, I spent the month traveling throughout China from Beijing, the capital, down in Central China, Chegtu, Chungking, and on the Yangtze. I thought it was a very important trip, a very incredible pilgrimage for me to take the Asiatic sources of the migrations of the native Americans into the Americas. I also felt a strange trepidation, almost a sense of fear to enter a country that has a billion people. And so, as I was entering, I kept remembering my grandfather who was a farmer in Puerto de Luna in a river valley in Nuevo Mexico. For some reason I kept using him as a guide, as a mentor, who was lending me his strength to go into that country, strange and foreboding, and a new country for me in many ways. And so my grandfather became the guide because he is in many ways like the Chinese rural peasant who is very much like our Hispanic peasant who worked on the land in the small ranchos and pueblos. They look the same—small, feisty, withered old men working the land. Also I had a friend, Cruz, from Taos Pueblo from New Mexico. I had visited with him a lot and hunted with him years ago when I was a young man.

81

During my trip to China, I had a lot of dreams. In many ways they revealed interesting symbols to me and answers I was searching for. One of the first dreams I had was that Cruz came to speak to me and also to serve as a guide like my grandfather. And this gave me the courage that I needed to approach the country and the people, and to look for the symbols and those little secrets that I seemed to be searching for in the culture and in the people and in the land.

When I came back from China a month later, I went up to Taos Pueblo to visit Cruz. I drove up to the pueblo to his home, and Tonito, his wife, answered the door. Right away she told me that Cruz had died. He had been sick, and we all expected it. But it was a shock. We started to talk and got around to, when did he die? And she told me that he died the exact day that I had my dream of him in China. So he had gone to China. My sense is that the dream is the flight of the soul, and who knows, but it may be more than that. It was just very interesting to me that in his last moments on earth before the transformation of his body, he visited me; he spoke to me again, and lent me his courage as a guide.

The turquoise bolo tie that you refer to that I am wearing is his. He had given it to me a year earlier, before his death. I had been up there in the summer and taken him—it's very common in the Indian culture as it is with the Mexicanos, to always take a little regalito or gift, o lo que sea, verdad?— and so I had taken him a couple of shirts, beautiful shirts to wear, and he gave me this bolo tie which I wear.

CG: You said also there was a dream of a truck, and also about a wall and bricks. I would like to hear them recounted bricfly.

RA: I had another very important dream. And these are dreams that I record that actually, in a way, I say came true. One of my dreams in China was that I thought I had bought a new, blue truck. Very merrily I came down the street, and I was traveling with a group of nineteen [Kellog Foundation] Fellows, and I told them, if you really want to see—with an emphasis on *see*—if you really want to see into the heart of China, what the people are really like, jump on my truck and I'll take you and show you. So I guess I was becoming, or thought I could become, a guide for my tour group. I say that modestly, but I think that was what the dream was saying. And some of them jumped on, and I remember in the dream just smiles. They were very happy, those who were willing to see China my way—a different way—not statistically, not how many people are there, not how many crimes are committed during a year, not numbers, but a different kind of seeing, a different kind of understanding. When I came home, I hadn't planned to buy a truck. I bought one that summer and the blue truck that I bought was identical to the truck that I was driving in the dream.

CG: A very short interruption here. You speak of the blue truck and the blue guitar in *Heart of Aztlan.* Is this in any way an allusion to Picasso's blue guitar that inspired Wallace Stevens' poem? Because, in that poem, Wallace Stevens says, "I am the blue guitar," somewhere in the middle.

RA: I read Wallace Stevens a lot when I was a student. I think he is one of the major poets of the imagination, let's say during our generation and the generation preceding that. Our time, let's say. So there is obviously, in *Heart of Aztlan,* an interplay with *The Man with the Blue Guitar.* And the blue guitar is an instrument of poetry and the imagination. More than that, I think the color blue in the blue guitar is symbolic of other things: The blue Mexican sky, the heavens, and also the realm of imagination.

CG: May I bring you to your third dream in China—of the great wall.

RA: Oh, the third dream! My wife and I had been talking a lot about building a fence around the front of our home in Albuquerque, and one of the dreams I had in China was that I met the contractor who helped me build our adobe home there about ten years ago. I said, "I want to build this fence." And he said, "Fine, let's do it." But the brick we saw in my dream were bricks that were made of Chinese characters, and since I don't read Chinese and he doesn't read Chinese, they were incomprehensible. He said, "I can't do this; I can't build a wall with Chinese character blocks." ¡Ni modo! So we didn't get the wall built. The deal fell through.

I came back to Albuquerque in the summer and thought more and more about the wall. I finally got, not my original contractor, but a guy that happened to come through the neighborhood and gave me a good deal on the wall. We got to work on it. And he designed an unusual wall in tiers, that has a sculptured effect of a Mayan pyramid or temple. Very strangely, people remarked about it. It's stucco, adobe-colored so it looks like an adobe wall. People came by and the first remarks were—I remember them precisely because I had such a laugh out of them—people would say, "You know, that looks like an Egyptian wall." And the second remark was, "You know, that looks like an Aztec wall from Mexico." None of them were saying it's a typical New Mexico wall. And it isn't. My old contractor came by, looked at it, and he said, "Is that your Chinese wall?" So somehow he had also worked his way into my dream, and there was a relationship.

CG: Pregunta: What is the relevance and relationship of archetypes in dreams and archetypes in myths to personal and social integration? Is there a focus, so that dreams relate more to personal integration and myth more to social integration? You seem to relate personal with social integration; what is the relationship between archetypes in dreams and archetypes in myths?

RA: The nature of the question is one that would require a great deal of time and thought to put your ideas in order and respond to it. But I really think that my answer to the first question would somehow be "Yes, that dreams have a greater relevance to personal integration because the dream is more personal." Although having given you just those three examples of dreams already, I don't know if dreams are that much personal because there is what I call the flight of the soul. If another soul can come in to me or visit me, then how personal is it really? . . . and then if there is some later kind of a correlation of that dream and another reality.

CG: We are our relationships. We define ourselves in terms of relationships.

RA: What will happen, I think, is that the myth will feed the dream and the dream will feed the myth in terms of energy and re-creation. But clearly in your question, I would also say that the myth has to do with that social, communal integration because the myth belongs to the community. It belongs to *the* people in any way you choose to define that communal group.

CG: Besides dream and myth, where else is archetype found in literature and experience?

RA: I think it depends on how you define the archetype. My sense has always been to define the archetype as a primal symbol. And that primal symbol would be available to all of us throughout mankind's history on earth. It is in the creation of art that we take those primal symbols or those archetypal symbols and infuse them into art. So that, I guess, what they become is a reflection that then speaks back to us because so many of those come from the subconscious. Sometimes we are not clearly aware of the use of archetypal symbols on other planes, or conscious planes.

CG: Luis Leal tells us that we must create myth to enter into universalism. ["The Problem of Identifying Chicano Literature." *The Identification and Analysis of Chicano Literature.* Ed. Francisco Jiménez. New York: Bilingual

Press, 1979. 4.] You have often spoken of the need to create myth. What do
you mean when you say that we must create myth? Make up stories of gods
and people in fairy tales? Or should we study world mythology, especially
native American mythology to which we may relate, and then open ourselves
to our collective consciousness in order to focus on archetypal symbol? It
sounds pretty abstract. What do you mean when you say we must create
myth? How do you create myth?

RA: I think the key here is that really all of these would fit. We should all
engage in the study of world mythology because that has an integrating sense
to it. When we discover that there are points of contact to other world myths,
we become sure of ourselves and say, "well because our particular mythology
comes clothed in a certain garment, it's not so strange because it will have
points of reference in contact to other mythologics." The key, when we say
we have to create myth, has to do with a collective memory. If we all share a
collective memory that has a biological base to it, then we share with everyone on earth and everyone who has preceded us, those points of contact,
points of reference, and we also share that archetypal pool. So it is very
important—given my particular bias or opinion or how I am—to understand
that collective reservoir, that collective memory and to find in it those pure
symbols, those archetypal symbols.

CG: How do you get in touch with this common reservoir of the collective
unconscious?

RA: Well, there are many ways to do it I guess, the most popular way
would be to meditate. To pray. To fast. To think. Also, in an artistic way, I
think here is where I get a big kick out of being a writer, being an artist,
because it is my process of writing that becomes a kind of meditation in
which I begin to tap myself. The archetypes reside in me, and in that process
of writing and thinking the story and energizing myself and using the energy
of the story, I begin to find those archetypals in me and, as I said earlier,
infuse them into the story. When I say we must create myth, I think that what
I mean by that is that we often look at mythology as if it happened in the
distant past. We say, "The Greeks had their mythology, and the Toltecs and
Aztecs of MesoAmerica had their mythology. Isn't that interesting. It's all in
the past, it's gone." We tend to view myth as static. What I am saying is that
it is not static. It's working in us even now. Because those same archetypals
that were discovered by the ancient people are in us today. And it is the
creation of myth and that reference to that collective pool that we all carry

inside of us that re-energizes us and makes us more authentic. If part of the search is for the authentic self in us, then those archetypals and symbols are clear messages that begin to define the authentic self.

CG: Luis Leal told me that, in his opinion, you, Miguel Méndez-M., Ron Arias, and Tomás Rivera are the leaders in the creation of myth (especially you and Méndez). How do you understand this? . . . And you say that you've never seen Rivera as particularly working in myth?

RA: I've taught Rivera's work, and I admire it. I teach it every semester: ". . . *y no se lo tragó la tierra.*" I teach it more from an existentialist point of view.

CG: Yes . . . defining himself. The little boy is under the house, at the end. Other children say they see "a man under the house." This perhaps could be understood as his having gone back into himself to find freedom and break with former structures . . . that he finally integrated himself at the point of transcendence. That may be what Luis Leal is referring to. Just as Arias is dealing with a point of transcendence, at the point of approaching death. The old man reconciled himself and came to peace and terms with reality. You have here this young man on a quest. Here he is trapped with the old institutions and forms and is breaking away from them. I don't know if that is necessarily mythical, but at any rate, it is interesting that you have not seen Rivera from that point of view.

RA: I haven't seen him . . . I haven't seen ". . . *y no se lo tragó la tierra"* as a work that actively engages the presentation of a myth that we all know and understand—or say, the work gropes to understand—infused again into the story he tells. Certainly the house is an archetypal symbol. But just to have archetypal symbols and to use them and to know how to use them doesn't make the writer an active participant in the creation of myth.

CG: How about Méndez and Arias? Do you see them as active in this development of myth?

RA: I can't speak well to Méndez's work because I haven't studied it enough to say something useful. Arias, I see very clearly in the stream of what we call magical realism which has a tremendous sense of playfulness with myth, but is concerned also with presentations of realities.

CG: Do you see your approach to myth as eclectic drawing from Jung, Freud, Lévi-Strauss, Cassirer, and others, or is there a focus and preference for one of these approaches to myth?

RA: I think my approach is eclectic. I have probably read, at one time or another, these philosophers, psychologists, cultural anthropologists, but I have never found myself following any particular school of thought. Although, of course, if you have read my work and you know anything about the work of these thinkers, you would put me in Jung's camp immediately. And you would say, "Your work is Jungian," which is fine with me. But I don't read Jung as a bible every night. So it is eclectic and so much of it has a basis in the thought of men like these—thinkers. But I am also very much interested in just allowing myself to see things and to learn things. I like to go to different cultures, to different people, and look at their dance, their art work, the little things in their homes, and their stories . . . their cuentos. How do those describe their world view in the use of archetypal symbols. I guess I'm eclectic in the sense that I like to open myself up to experience. It's like opening myself up to that collective memory, and letting the impressions affect me, then I reflect on them and see. And then I also use them sometimes for not only thinking but for my work, for literature. I don't care very much if I am doing it correctly or incorrectly depending on Jung or Freud, or Lévi-Strauss.

CG: Do you use Northop Frye's "Structure of Literary Types" as a map, as it were, for developing your novels sometimes?

RA: No, never.

CG: A question from a student (R.M.). I am Catholic. I read you and other Chicano writers caricaturing the church. For example, your character of Father Cayo in *Heart of Aztlan*. And these writers point out how much the church has collaborated with other institutions to exploit the people. Are you asking me to reject the church and/or my faith? Is this rejection of the Catholic church/faith essential to finding and defining my freedom? I'm thinking in part of the young man in ". . . *y no se lo tragó la tierra*." Are you asking me to search for some kind of natural religion based on myths and nature?

RA: Well, I would start first of all by saying I am not asking this student to do anything. Certainly, I am not asking him to reject his religion or embark on a new search for a natural religion. I think the nature of his question might suggest that he is asking himself whether he should do that. As to the church, it would take a long time to describe my personal crisis of faith that I went through as a young man after having been raised a Catholic and in the church and having to come to my own view of the world and the integration that I wanted in terms of the authentic self. I didn't think the church was providing me everything that I needed. I also think that in many respects the church has been an institution that to be quite blunt, has been repressive in the lives of people. I meet many people who talk about having a sense of this institution, that is very important and intricately tied in with faith, being a force that, rather than liberating self, represses self. And since I think that's part of my job as a writer—to liberate myself and to search out what is the most authentic to me—I did have years of questioning the basis of this very fixed and dogmatic religion and then embarked on my own path. But I don't really proselytize for everybody to do that because religion is, I think, a question bound up with what you believe with faith.

CG: And that is ultimately the person. However, you would be saying, if I understand you, don't let the church or any other institution so lock you in that your freedom, your autonomy, your self-definition, ends up in constraints.

RA: Yes, I think so. It is like we live under a set of laws and governments—national, state and local governments—and we accept the rule of law, but that doesn't mean we are not constantly critical of it, or shouldn't be critical of it.

CG: Or that the only alternative is anarchy.

RA: Yes, or that the only alternative is anarchy. In search of a better world for everyone, we keep being critical of those laws that we impose on ourselves. And so, if the church is, indeed, for me one more institution that imposes a set of laws, I feel that I have the right also to be critical of that set of laws.

CG: A woman whom I knew in the movimiento years ago in L.A. asked last night about women in Chicano literature and your role. I understand that women once walked out on you during one of your presentations.

RA: No, I think women have never walked out on one of my presentations.

CG: That must have been a misapprehension on her part. I thank you for your clarification. Setting that aside, do you think of your writing as being concerned with women? Are you explicitly conscious and looking out for how women are portrayed in your writings in the evolving Chicano culture and the dynamics of their growth?

RA: I think so. Very obviously. In fact, I open myself to more critical thought on this subject because I don't think there is any other Chicano writer who has created as many strong women characters as I have. I think there were reservations with Ultima in *Bless Me, Ultima* for awhile. The Chicana in pursuing fulfillment of her own authentic self looked at Ultima and said: "I somehow don't seem to find a model that fits me if I want to be a doctor, attorney, or professional woman." And the only thing I can say to that is—in a sense it is a limited view, because I was writing about a certain time in our culture, in a very rural New Mexican setting which had a very traditional role for both the men and the women, and I was trying to reflect that. So I could not make Ultima an aspiring Chicana attorney and have any kind of a novel that I was writing of that time. On the other hand, in her own time, she acts with tremendous power in the world of men, so I think it's fair to remember that.

CG: You spoke of creating other powerful women characters.

RA: Well, I just finished the novel, *The Legend of La Llorona* which has to do with Malinche, in which I suggest a new motivation for Malinche. That is, that she did not act out of impulse rage and jealousy when Cortez jilts her, and then she has to make a decision about whether she gives up her son. In this case, I describe two boys that she has. (I play around with whatever the facts are). She had to decide whether she would give them up to Cortez, who will take them to the court of Spain where they will be held up to ridicule, or to sacrifice them as warriors of a new resistance. And so the motivations I ascribe to Malinche are, I think, much more noble in the sense of how we describe classical tragedy. I have also done a screen play, that hasn't been produced, which has as the central character a young girl, Rosalinda. So I continue, I think, to attack the portrayal [of stereotypes] as best I can.

CG: A quick question, just to satisfy my curiosity. What is the symbolism of the steel pins in *Heart of Aztlan?*

RA: It comes out of part of the folk belief that you ward off a bruja, or a witch, by making the cross of the alfileres or little pins that have been blessed at the church. And to me it was just a common part of some of the belief that I grew up with, and I thought it would be very clear for most Chicanos that grew up with that body of what we call folklore and I call a system of belief. The way you trap a witch in your house is by inviting her in and then putting a crucita of los pins on the door, and then she cannot pass because they symbolize, of course, the cross of Christ. Whatever evil the bruja has that has come to your home cannot pass against the cross.

CG: One closing question. You came here to Floricanto Cinco organized by Aztleca. The academic part of the program organized by the university did not take place on Friday. You knew ahead of time that it would not take place, and yet you came. Why did you come?

RA: Well, I am very interested in what's happening across the Southwest. Something started with the Chicano movement—what we call quite simply the rediscovery of our Indian heritage, and I think it's taking on a new urgency and a new importance for us. I have felt in the recent past few years that this is happening more and more, and it's happening in a very positive way. So I not only wanted to meet the people here but also in a way, to make contact with this renewal and this sense of search that we have been going through and discovering. It also ties into those archetypal symbols. How are we using those materials and symbols that came out of the past for us in our very contemporary world?

CG: You think you came, in part, for yourself. You wanted to experiment with part of your own development and growth perhaps.

RA: I think I came because, since I began writing and since I first published in 1972, which is a number of years ago, I was very much in tune with this world that we had to discover which was that second part of our nature for those of us who relate to our Indian heritage. There were, in the beginning, some people who opposed it because they thought it was too much of that fairy tale mythology, you see, that had no relevance to our life. Now it pleases me to see the young people, community people, and other people, continuing that kind of search and carrying it forward and re-establishing their roots in that very important other part of ourselves. The search for that authentic self again can't take place in only one campo, in one camp. It has to be eclectic. It has to begin to draw in all the sources that have fed our history.

Of Cuentistas, Myth, and the Magic of Words: An Interview with Rudolfo Anaya

Paul Vassallo / 1985

From *Lector*, 5.1 (1988): 9–21. Reprinted by permission of publisher.

With the publication of *Bless Me, Ultima* in 1972, Rudolfo Anaya assumed a leading role in the world of Chicano literature. He has followed the storytelling tradition of his forebears, weaving together the mythology and the geography of the Southwest to form a tapestry that is uniquely Chicano.

This interview was recorded for the Archive of Hispanic Literature on Tape, a collection of the Library of Congress begun some 43 years ago. Up to now, the Archive has focused primarily on authors from Spain, Portugal, and the Caribbean. In recognition of the emergence of the literature emanating from North Americans of Hispanic descent, it has recently started collecting interviews with Chicano writers.

In addition to being an admirer of Rudy's work and my having edited a small book about Rudy and his writing, my wife, Bonita, and I love Rudy and his wife, Pat, as friends. Thus I feel that this interview is more of a conversation among *compadres than a scholarly discussion by a noted author and a dispassionate interviewer or literary critic.*

Frank Waters, in an appreciative footnote included in *The Magic of Words,* writes that "Rudolfo Anaya's writing achieves a reconciliation between his natural feeling and acquired intellectual knowledge. Anaya never forgets his childhood. Almost everything he has written casts back to his earliest years in Santa Rosa, and bears the stamp of his Spanish-Indian heritage."

Paul Vassallo: Rudy, you have said that to you, all writing is biographical. To introduce you to our readers perhaps you can tell us about your formative years—the years of the "rites of passage" that are so frequently reflected in your writing. Who were some of the key role models that had an impact on your life, and, thereby, your writing?

Rudolfo Anaya: My formative years—my years as a child—were spent in Santa Rosa, here in New Mexico. I grew up in a small town, the village of

Pastura on the eastern open plain of New Mexico, the land we call the *llano*. And by age two or three, I guess, my family had moved to Santa Rosa. The big sheep and cattle ranches of the area were not employing as many people as they used to, and my father's work was normally in that area: with livestock. I suppose that what has interested me most in looking back on my life as a child has been the key elements that are involved in my rites of passage—growing into manhood, and also in the area of formation—how is a person formed? The people are the most important element, I think. The people that I grew up with—my family and the community that was part also of my family, a very big extended family which included aunts, uncles, *primos*—people who always seemed related to us, even though we didn't call them uncles or aunts. In those small villages and ranches, the relationship of people is very strong. I think those same people who had such a gift for storytelling . . . looking back, I have always given them a great deal of credit, because in listening to their stories, I have always thought that my own imagination was sparked; I became a storyteller following in the tradition of those *cuentistas.*

I think the land was very important. I grew up in the Pecos River Valley, and knew the river intimately as a young boy, playing there all day long with friends, hiking up and down the river, staying out a day or two at a time, living off the land. And also knowing the *llano*. It was a sheep- and cattle-ranching area. Trips out into the *llano* put one in touch with that landscape.

The whole idea of religion is very important, I think. I grew up in a Catholic household, attended the Catholic Church rituals—mass. There was always something very immediate about what we call the emotions of life if you grow up in a small town. Death seems always to be closer. In *Bless Me, Ultima,* I deal with the deaths of three people and I think in my own childhood, death was a very important emotion shared by families and communities. I grew up right when World War II was ending, so there was also that spectre of death, the death outside our community that caused death to the young men of the village.

The whole area of mysticism that people have asked about in my work, especially my first novel, *Bless Me, Ultima,* comes in part out of those ingredients I have mentioned. The folk belief that there is a power of evil that can incarnate itself in different forms is partly out of the Catholic world and partly out of the Native American indigenous world. And by the time I get to be a writer years later, when I'm at the University of New Mexico doing undergraduate work, and thinking that I can put all this in poems and stories,

I look back at my childhood and discover that it's got the richest source of materials that I can possibly use for creating stories. And so, I begin to deal with some of those elements that I've just mentioned, you know? How does a young boy grow up; how is he affected by his family and the traditions and ceremonies around him; what about that whole belief system that has to do with magic that normally had not been written too much [about] in what we call American literature. It was very accessible to us; it was part of our life. What is our relationship to God if we begin to question those beliefs that we were taught when we were young. I think that became part of my inquiry into the nature of things, and certainly shows up in my work. Well, I've listed a few elements there. I'm not sure if I've covered your question.

PV: Yes, I think you have. I did want to have you touch a little bit, perhaps, on some key role models. You did mention uncles and relatives, but perhaps other role models that either influenced the beginning of your writing or that you used as actual models in your writings.

RA: Well, the role model that would have influenced me to become a writer would have been the storyteller, and there is no one particular person that I can point to there. It seems like culture to me, if I look back and remember, is rich in the tradition of the storyteller. Almost everybody was a storyteller.

PV: Actually storytelling has quite a role in both Chicano literature as well as Native American literature because that has been the mode of transmitting the stories.

RA: It's extremely important. The history has been transmitted through the oral tradition. We haven't had the access to education and therefore the training and publications, and part of the contemporary movement reflects that. But the history of the people, of the villages, the traditions that had to do with baptisms, marriage, death and the burial ceremonies, the *velatorios* (the wakes); all of these were transmitted orally. So you listened to them. I really grew up in a world that taught you to listen and to record and to remember.

PV: Do you feel that to a certain degree, perhaps the evolution of Chicano literature will have an impact on the continued existence of storytelling? Do you feel that, because there is a rich body of literature evolving, that this may have a negative effect on the continued existence or presence of storytelling as a medium?

RA: I doubt it. I think that as long as a people continue to meet, at a party or around the kitchen table or informally or where you work, you're always going to have the impulse to tell stories, to create stories, to embellish or just to pass on what is happening in the community. On the other hand, for *our* community, I think it's very vital that we now have access to the printed word—an access, I think, that we have created ourselves; it hasn't been given easily to us—because the dissemination of the literature is wider and there is a sharing. We are not only limited now to our particular little village or family; we can share with the Chicano experience in Texas and California and Colorado, in the Midwest, in Washington, so that's very important to us.

PV: One question that I know you have been asked frequently in previous interviews, but yet I feel is important: what language did you speak at home and in the neighborhood? And what impact did this language have on your writing, or even perhaps on your starting to write, not just what you wrote?

RA: The language that I spoke at home was Spanish. Until the time I was six and was sent to grade school, to the first grade, I spoke only Spanish. Both my father and my mother spoke Spanish—all my immediate family and community. In fact, as I look back and think about those rural villages of New Mexico in which a Mexican population lived, that was the only language, and in fact, the lifestyle of those villages had, I think remained largely unchanged since the coming of the Spaniard and the Mexican to New Mexico. Even the coming of the Anglo-American in the mid-nineteenth century did not change the use of language in those villages. All of the people I knew in the villages, like Puerto de Luna where my grandparents lived, spoke only Spanish. I suppose they had to deal in part [in English] when they went to town to buy things for their farms and their ranches.

But in a sense, I think what you're asking me is the most important element that we have to address as a community of people that want to transmit our values and remain an identifiable community, and that is the language. I knew very quickly when I started going to the university that in order to compete in the university I had to learn English, so I really concentrated on it and went after it. So when I began to write, it was somewhat normal for me to write in English. I had dominated the language more than Spanish. But at home in the community, in the barrio later on when we moved to Albuquerque, the language was all Spanish and the unique mixture that we have in the Southwest of Spanish and English: we borrow words back and forth. You have your bilingual element occurring all the time.

PV: I would assume from my own experience growing up in a bilingual environment where the "foreign language" predominates, that you really were not encouraged outside of the home to use the Spanish. I mean, the school system did not encourage you to use the Spanish, although that is changing. But when *you* were growing up. . . .

RA: Well, in my generation, you're absolutely correct. No, there was no encouragement in all my grade school and secondary school to ever use Spanish, to study it, to learn it—to be *proud* of it, because that is an important element. Again, if one looks at the relationship of the Anglo-American and the Chicano communities in the Southwest, particularly in the state that I think I know a little bit better, in New Mexico, language is such a crucial element of the culture, and it carries such an important part of the culture. In fact, some people go so far as to say that the culture is language: that if you don't have the language, you've lost the culture. It seems to me that since the mid-nineteenth century, one of the attempts that has been in the making has been not to encourage the use of Spanish in the world of business and the public world and in the world of professions. And this is very obvious in the grade school and the secondary school levels, where many instructors would ridicule their students who did speak Spanish, and sometimes punish them. It's part of the background of this area where you have a different culture that has just arrived in order to impose its will and its power; it tries to get you very quickly to change into its language and to give up yours. That is, I think, a technique that is historic in the sense that we can see it operating in many places in the world. I think what has happened in New Mexico is that the Hispanic communities—the villages—have resisted that complete assimilation into the Anglo-American culture and have also resisted a complete assimilation into the use of English. So we have a bilingual population and, therefore, bilingual writers. I think most of the writers that I know of, the Chicano writers, use a bilingual element in their writing, or can do it; it's readily accessible to us.

PV: In terms of the inspiration that you were provided in your home life, in the life of the neighborhood, in the life of New Mexico, what other sources of inspiration did you have? Obviously the language per se is the primary source of inspiration; as you said, "language is culture." But what other sources of inspiration did you have, such as authors or books that you may have read, and what kind of impact did these have especially on your early writing—as you started writing?

RA: In the context of our community, it seems to me the only source of inspiration was really the family. In large [part], our parents were the ones who encouraged us to continue in education, and who gave us the financial support—not only the emotional encouragement, but the financial support. In terms of role models, we didn't have any. And again I'm speaking of my generation that grew up in the fifties and the sixties. We never had role models in high school; we had absolutely no literature written by Chicanos. That was true when I was at the university. At the university level, I got a B.A. and an M.A. degree in literature studying in the English Department, and never once read a novel by a Chicano. So there was no encouragement to pursue that literature or to learn about it. There was really a great vacuum there—in part also a great longing, because we knew from the context of our own tradition of the storyteller, that there were a lot of people out there that were very creative. But in education, it's the printed word that matters, and so I read as much as I could of world literature and American literature, and that satisfied a great part of my love of literature.

When I went to write, I found that a lot of those novels that I had read—the American novels—really didn't quite suit my interest and I didn't know why. When the Chicano movement came around in the 1960s, and there was this explosion of creative work, literary work, people with the same yearnings that I had, the same desires to write about their own life from the inside point of view, from a real knowledge point of view, it was a struggle because the models were not there; the works we should have read were not there. So it was, in effect, creating a contemporary literature that would describe us in a contemporary sense and describe our history, our values, our towns, our families, our barrios, and all the passions and emotions and joy and grief that we attribute to characters once we put them in fiction. And at the same time to rediscover that we did indeed have a link to history: that once we began to look at the oral tradition, we found that it was very rich. Some people began to look into lost manuscripts and began to find novels that were indeed sitting around in old trunks in houses. Newspapers of the past began to reveal a great wealth of material that our forefathers—the Chicanos who came before us—had published. It was just that somehow that historic link had almost been broken. I think if my generation, if the writers of the Chicano movement had not come when they did, it is quite possible that we would have seen a much more rapid assimilation of the Chicano population into the mainstream culture. In effect, I've always thought that the Chicano movement of the sixties throughout the Southwest—everywhere there were Chicano populations—was not only a retrieval of our self-image, our historic image, and not only a need for political and social justice, and not only a renaissance of creativity in the community, but it was also putting the brakes on the assimilation process and saying, "Wait a minute, we need to look very closely at our community and make some very hard decisions." And if nothing else, if the Chicano movement has no other value in history, I think *that* will be one value: that it put a stop to things and began to use its own materials to create art, music, literature, sculpture, and everything else.

So that was a very important time, I think, for me, because I published my first novel in 1972, which was right at the peak of that analysis that was going out throughout our communities. We were asking ourselves who we were and where we wanted to go.

PV: So in effect, you are saying that the oral tradition had limitations in expanding the level of consciousness, so the evolution of literature was very important to the Chicano movement.

RA: The oral tradition had limitations in this sense: that the rules of the game had changed. By a hundred years after the Anglo-American culture comes into the Southwest and takes over the major institutions that affect every person's life—the most important of which is education—once you take over those institutions, the oral tradition is not strong enough to deal with them. The rules have changed. And if the schools are teaching only English, and only English and Anglo-American history, then they exert a great deal of influence on these communities. So we had to learn the rules of the new game and learn to play by the rules; at the same time trying to preserve what we knew our culture is like—our own traditions, our own history—and demand indeed that that history of our people be a part of the educational system.

PV: Your strength in literature has been primarily reflected through prose, through the novel, but you have also published poetry. What can you tell us about the evolution of your style, your approach and the thematic development in your writings?

RA: I think in the first three novels that I published, *Bless Me, Ultima; Heart of Aztlan; Tortuga;* the themes are possibly not that varied or different. I do follow certain themes throughout the novels: the rites of passage, the coming into new awareness, the mythic element underlying—underpinning, so to speak—the Hispanic and Native American culture. More and more of a search in my Native American indigenous roots, which was part of the Chicano movement, to understand our history and to put it in a correct, truthful context.

I think, stylistically . . . in a way, I've always been changing, I've always tried to do new works. Not only improve my writing, but writing is one of the most fascinating occupations there is; I was about to say one of the most *playful* things we do. Because there's so much that you can do with it. You never learn completely; there's always new ways to work with the craft of writing, and I've always tried to keep an eye open for experimentation and challenge. So I've done not only novels, but short novels. I did *The Adventures of Juan Chicaspatas* last year, which is a long epic poem. I'm working on a new novel now, and I'll be challenging myself in terms of technique and style to try new things. So it's never remained at one spot. If I had to say what is the one central theme that seems to be beneath my work, it would be probably the same answer that most Chicano writers would give in this country today, and that is to project a truthful image, given whatever context you're working with, of our community. We're very committed to the importance of literature in acting as a mirror which reflects the community, which reflects the values, which reflects the history. And quite often our feeling is that we can do it better because we (meaning those of us that are writers that are Chicanos) have lived with them.

PV: I think, to follow up on this last bit of discussion, there has been an increased awareness, in this Anglo-American society, of a Hispanic society and culture which has had an even longer history in North America. Yet you are considered a Chicano author or a purveyor of Chicano life and culture. How do you feel that Chicano literature, as distinct from what has been called Hispanic literature in general, has evolved in the past decade, and what do you see as the prognosis for the next decade? In responding to this question, could you touch on what you consider to be the distinctive characteristics of Chicano literature and what major trends exist in the product of Chicano authors? For example, the departure of Chicano literature from what has been considered in American literature as a "regional" literature, that is, the literature of the Southwest. How is Chicano literature different from that type of literature? And are there any major strengths that this type of literature has, and are there any weaknesses?

RA: Well, let me begin by defining some of the terms that you use. I don't use the word "Hispanic" to characterize me or my writing. I use the word "Chicano." Yes, I am Hispanic, because I come from a culture that is Spanish-speaking and has its history in the Southwest from Mexico, and then from Spain and the other Mediterranean cultures. The word "Chicano" to me, and the reason I use it, means a particular group under that Hispanic umbrella. More specifically, it means the Mexican-American group and those of us who believed in the Chicano movement and worked in it and created some of our early works in it, made a commitment to the image which the word "Chicano" seems to define. And that image has to do with our commitment to understanding ourselves not only as Hispanics—as people of Spanish and Mexican origins—but as people who also share in the Native American origin and the Native American heritage. Our history is part Indian. So that was part of our commitment, and I think that's what "Chicano" defines for us. It's not at all, as some people would want to believe, necessarily a word only of radicalism or a word that has only political connotations. It also has more important connotations that define a certain community of people.

It is a regional literature, if we consider that Chicano is primarily a southwestern community. As a regional literature, what does it have to offer the mainstream Anglo-American literature? Well, the answer is what every other regional literature has offered. The South has offered and continues to offer its regional perspective. So does the literature of New York City or the Eastern Seaboard, so does the literature of the West. I think if the country is really going to be responsive and interested in its communities, it will have to be as responsive to the literature of the Chicanos as it has been to other regions. There is nothing lacking, from my point of view, or making the literature anything less that it is, when we say it's regional. All regional literature has the ability within itself to create works that will universalize the human experience. So that's why I'm not concerned with the "regional" label.

PV: But there exists in Chicano literature a kind of departure from the common element that exists in the regional literature within American literature, wouldn't you say?

R.A.: Oh yes, of course, because the culture that it's portraying is so unique. It's a culture that has a 400-year history here in the Southwest, a culture that shares from the Spanish and Mexican and Native American traditions and religions and world views. So you have a very unique mixture when you talk about Chicano literature.

PV: It had to break a barrier: whereas Southern literature, for instance, was already being built on a certain knowledge base, Chicano literature is breaking away from it.

RA: Well, because of the historical context. If you look at the South, you can look at certain elements that defined that region and its people and their values, but the language is still English. They have a connection to the Eastern Seaboard United States all the way to Maine, and to the mother country which is Great Britain and to northern Europe, and to the language base.

Our history and our context is completely different. We are historically tied to Mexico, that has been feeding us spiritually and linguistically for over 400 years, and with that context of the Mexican experience is the experience of the Native American, whether that experience be in Mexico or here in the Southwest.

Stylistically, the Chicano literature has a lot to offer because it reflects that world view, which is very, very different from the Anglo-American world view. Our ties are not only to different social and political realities; spiritually we reflect different myths, which has been one of my concerns in literature: to bring out the myths that are an important part of the core of the world view. Stylistically, we are closer to elements of magical realism than the different kind of clean, hard prose that has to do with Puritanism. So the differences to me are fascinating, and it's part of the reason why I think we're so important in terms of not only national literature, but international.

PV: In this paper, "The Dynamics of Myth in the Creative Vision of Rudolfo Anaya," Henri Calamadrid states that, "The universal thrust of Anaya's creative vision is based in myth, which he defines impressionistically as 'the truth and the heart'." How do you feel you have contributed through your writings to the understanding of that myth? How have you elaborated on it? Can you start by defining the myth that you represent through your writing?

RA: Well, I think we've probably gotten into the area that I'd much rather spend our hour talking about—the element of myth in fiction, particularly my work. I suppose there is no one myth that I am really talking about. Really, my interest has been to look at the world view of my community, and at the core of that world view are essential values: how we relate to each other, to the family, to the earth, elements of faith, elements of respect, and I could go on. It seems to me that all world views, at the root, touch the mythology of mankind. What culture does, simply, is somehow to filter that and make it specific to your time in history. And touching the myth was important, because to bring the myth and to make it part of the fiction, part of the story, means that you're tying into your past and to your collective memory and to your history, and reminding people of the sources of their inspiration, and their values. So it's not just one myth that we have to explore, it's the myths of our world view. Which ones are more important to me? The Native American myths. Why? Because it seems to me we already know, if we receive a liberal education in the Western tradition, the mythology of the Greeks, of the Romans, of the Catholic Church and later of the Protestant Reformation. We know the Judeo-Christian tradition. So we know all about mythology. What was lacking for our community, it seems to me, was to be in touch with Native American mythology, and that would complete the picture.

What does mythology have to do with a person? Or, if I may be so daring, what should a person feel like after they've read one of my novels in which I begin to explore a Native American mythology and bring it out in the best way I can to fit the story? Probably my answer would be: a shock of recognition; that for the first time you are really seeing your true self somehow reflected in the novel. And that's been exactly what has happened when people have talked to me about *Bless Me, Ultima.* They say, "Well, I don't understand the Legend of the Golden Carp (that I have in the novel), but it was intriguing; tell me about it. I think they understand it in Judeo-Christian terms, and how they really want to understand it is out of that Native American indigenous tradition that I'm writing in. And that's fulfilling to me as a writer, when people begin to touch those truths in the heart that I am after in myself: what am I really like at the core, you know?, what are the traditions that have fed all of that history and culture that formed me? Well, it is certainly not only Anglo-American tradition, and it is certainly not only a Judeo-Christian tradition. It has to do also with Native American indigenous tradition. Once I begin to put all of those together, then I think I am a more complete person.

PV: Is that why, then, there exists such an element of magic in the writing?

RA: The element of magic might come probably from the fact that the Native American tradition considers its oral tradition to be sacred, you know? The passing on of important ceremonies is extremely important. And when you only have the word to pass them on, the word becomes sacred. So it has a more powerful content than the printed word, because the printed word doesn't require as much of you; it loses part of its sacredness. The other part of the magic may have to do with reality, and, that is, many of the Chicano writers of the Chicano movement were not as much interested in that sacredness of the word as they were that the word was powerful because it could refute a political and a social reality that had been imposed on us. Or if not refute, at least struggle against and fight and create its own reality. So either way, I think in either camp, when you look at the power of the word, there's some truth to both. From one tradition we learn it as the word being sacred, and, given the context of our contemporary reality, it has a power to create our own image, and that means struggling against whatever oppression is keeping you from that true image.

PV: Do you see any similarity in the approach to magic that exists in the writings of such Latin American authors as García Márquez and others, and your writing?

RA: I think in some of the Chicano writers it comes out more obviously than in others. Certain of my writings have been placed in that camp.

And I think [the similarity] is very obvious, because García Márquez shares with us that Hispanic background in language. In his case, the indigenous tradition is a bit different, but it's also a tradition that has a long history in contemplating and defining the world of spirituality, the world view.

PV: It's a mixture of the Hispanic and the mestizo, isn't it, which really is similar, although within different geographical contexts.

RA: Yes, and his happens to be, I think, more of that Gulf Coastal area, more Caribbean. But, yes, the geographic positions of this entire Latin American culture are what create the differences and variations. But at the core will be what we find out about our indigenous myths.

PV: You are primarily noted for your novels, which include *Bless Me, Ultima; Heart of Aztlan; Tortuga;* and *The Legend of La Llorona.* Your other books include *Cuentos: Tales from the Hispanic Southwest, Cuentos chicanos, A Ceremony of Brotherhood, 1680–1980, The Silence of the Llano,* and, most recently, *The Adventures of Juan Chicaspatas.* In spite of such a great publishing record, I have discovered that your work is not represented in most of the major research libraries in this country. Now, do you see this as an example of the difficulty for Chicano literature to be accepted as an element of American literature, or is this perhaps reflective of the problems of the distribution of books published by small presses? Do you foresee broader acceptability and a wider audience through publishing by some of the bigger, well established firms?

RA: I think it's a factor of both elements, possibly more. Most of the Chicano work of the sixties and seventies and actually to date, to 1985, has been published by small presses, and most of these presses are small Chicano presses. They don't have the distribution capability, so our work cannot get out and be as widely distributed as we would like. I think, on the other hand, there is a resistance in the mainstream culture, and this has become most obvious, I imagine, in the past five years: a resistance to any kind of ethnic pluralism. It seems to me that this factor might also be influencing that lack of access to our work in the wider culture. The fact that there are forces in the society that want to make the society very homogenous with a certain set of values—and that English is the only language by which we can express ourselves in this country—seem to me a part of the reactionary character of this society. And it's one, I think, that we are committed to struggle against simply because we are committed to our culture and our own world view and our values.

I don't know if all that is going to change. I think the nature of political times changes and so it might ease up sometime in the distant future. And through more distribution and more education, people will become more aware of our community of people and begin to look into our literature, which is an obvious first step when we want to learn about people and about different societies. We can't visit all the societies in the world, but we can certainly read their literature.

I don't see any attempt at all on the part of big commercial publishers to publish Chicano literature. That is a most baffling question of our time. When we have already proven that we have writers of national stature whose works would be competitive in the marketplace, there is still no interest. I think most people would say that that's a sad picture of publishing in our country, in our literary world—that the marketplace and the bottom line influence so much what will be published, that we don't stand a chance. Big commercial publishers don't see us as being able to make the bucks for them in New York and the big cities, so they're not interested.

The other element is a harder one to prove and one almost doesn't want to think about it—the possibility that there is some kind of inherent racism in the publishers, and we simply cannot get past that. Of course, you hate to think that, but some writers have said that's the case and now have refused to even deal with the big publishers.

PV: Do you feel that they have some kind of sanitizing process that one would have to submit to—probably for all writers, but perhaps more so for those who may be considered "foreign" or "different"?

RA: I think so. I have no doubt that the editorial committees that get together say, "This novel has to sell 100,000 copies for us even to consider it, and, because it is set in New Mexico, written by a Chicano and has a lot of words in Spanish, and it may displease some of the libraries where we should expect to sell it, it just won't make it," and so they come down to a monetary conclusion, which is, I think, a sad commentary on publishing in this country.

Those of us who started with the small presses, the alternative presses in the country, continue to work with them and see a lot of future in that. Perhaps we have to educate the public to seek out the work of those small presses that aren't always at the drugstore counter or in the airport.

PV: Speaking of presses, I understand that the University of New Mexico Press is going to be publishing your journal of your trip to China. Isn't this somewhat of a departure from your style of writing so far? Or is it?

RA: Well, I remember, I told you earlier that I always keep challenging myself to do new things. I'm writing plays now: different kinds of plays with different subject matter. I was in China last year, in 1984, for a month, and all I did was keep a daily diary of my impressions. When I got back, UNM Press was very excited about the journal of a Chicano in China. I think that I'm the first Chicano who has ever gone to China and looking, again, for roots, for elements of myth. After all, the Asiatic mainland is the origin of the migrations to the New World, so there must be some connection there, also. The whole world eventually will connect, right?

PV: I hope so. Did you have some experiences that you have related in your journal that you wish to share with us?

RA: Well, I do. I don't know if we have the time to go into the journal. I was very interested in the dreams that I had in China, and recorded them. I was very interested in the fact that I needed mentors or guides to help me go through that fantastic country, and I found myself turning back again to my roots, to my grandfather, and a good friend of mine from Taos Pueblo, and they in a sense helped me go spiritually through China. I went to the lakes and ponds and saw the golden carp which I had already written about in *Bless Me, Ultima.* And just making connections—to their storytelling and to their folktales, to the use of the dragon that they use so much in their mythology. All those points of reference, I think, will be shown in the journal.

PV: Well, Rudy, I think we will conclude this interview. I do want to thank you very much for taking time out to do this.

Rudolfo Anaya
John F. Crawford / 1986

From *This Is About Vision: Interviews with Southwestern Writers,* eds. William Balassi, John F. Crawford, and Annie O. Eysturoy. University of New Mexico Press, 1990, 83–93. Reprinted by permission of publisher.

This interview with John Crawford took place in Rudolfo Anaya's office in May 1986.

Anaya: One of the most interesting experiences about coming to Albuquerque in the fifties was coming from a very small rural town into a big city *barrio* and being thrown into a completely different life-style. Recently, while attending the Writers of the Purple Sage Conference, it occurred to me that almost every writer there had shared a similar experience. No one lives in a small town any more; nearly all of us are city writers. Although I had all my upbringing in that small town, the majority of my life has been spent in the big city now. That's kind of shocking—we write about our roots that are close to the land, and then we get slapped with this new reality.

Crawford: In your novels there's a double move, from the llano to the small towns and then to the big city.

Anaya: I think it's a progression that has happened in New Mexico. Historically, after World War II you have that exodus from the small towns into the metropolitan areas, especially from the Mexican working community. The new professions were being opened up, the GI Bill was sending some of the veterans to the university, and my writing reflects that historical pattern.

Crawford: In *Heart of Aztlan* it sounds like the small factories were opening up in New Mexico and they were exploiting cheap labor where they could find it, and that would be a reason also.

Anaya: Absolutely.

Crawford: One particular way I remember you writing about the space you grew up in had to do with interior space: the public library in Santa Rosa.

Anaya: I would visit it periodically, starting at an early age, when I was in grade school. It was a little one-room library actually placed on top of the fire house on the first floor, where there was an old beaten up fire truck used on a volunteer basis when there was a fire in the town. We climbed up those rickety steps to the little room that was the library. That interests me too, you know, looking back at what was formative in my love of books.

Crawford: In your novels the formative influences seem to be the figures who represent wisdom and knowledge, like Ultima and Crispin. Were there real people like that in your life who would serve such a function, or are those characters a sort of metaphor or composite?

Anaya: I think it was a little bit of each. In our Hispanic culture there is a great deal of respect given to older people—and growing up in the forties as I did, the relationships that we had with older people were ones of trust. We listened to what they said and we learned from them. And these were specific people that I knew and held in awe. These fabulous *vaqueros* would come in from the llano and my father or brothers and I would visit them; to me, they were almost mythological figures, bigger than life. I think I felt the same way about teachers, because it was normal in our culture to be taught by anyone who was older and to give him or her respect. So when I came to write my novels, which basically have to do with a search for meaning or an archetypal journey, the person who can guide the hero turns out to be the older person not only out of the structure of myth as we know it but out of my background, out of my life. Those older people played very important roles. We believed that *curanderas* could cure; we saw them do it. We believed that there were evil powers that came to be represented by witches, because we lived in the universe where we saw those powers work.

Crawford: And also that things were animated with life, like Tortuga the mountain. There were places that had power.

Anaya: Most definitely. I think it's Clemente in *Heart of Aztlan* who recalls, "I remember there were times and certain places in the llano where I grew up where I would stand at this place and have a feeling of elation, a feeling of flying"—that's interesting, because there are *cuentos* or folk tales where you get these little stories about people who can fly—so in your mind you think, where does this power come from? Is it the power of imagination that we as a communal group are given by those older, wiser people, or can it actually be? So it was very interesting to deal with the power that the earth has to animate us—we *are* animated by the power of the earth—it is in Native American terms our Mother—it nurtures us, it gives us spirit and sustenance, and I guess if we're attuned enough or sensitive enough it can give us different *kinds* of powers. And so, coming out of that kind of complex universe where I grew up thinking of all these places, the river and the hills, having this life to them, this animation, it was very good not only for growing up but for the imagination, getting fed by that very spiritual process that was in the natural world around me.

Crawford: That must have come to you first in the *cuentos* themselves, the stories you would have heard while growing up. When did you start taking an interest in myth outside your own culture—was that in college— and where did this interest lead you?

Anaya: It was probably when I was an undergraduate here at UNM. We were guided to read Greek mythology. I wasn't really making the connections because I was looking at it as stories that had to do with another time and place. I think it wasn't until I turned more toward Native American mythology that I began to see that there are these points of reference that world myths have, that somehow speak to the center of our being, and connect us—to other people, to the myth, to the story, and beyond that to the historic process, to the communal group.

Crawford: You have a way of making the myths take on very specific roles in the novels. I'm thinking of the incredible way that the mountain and the boy interplay at the beginning of *Tortuga,* where the mountain actually moves and something in the boy moves. It must have taken a great deal of trial and error to find out artistic ways to make the myths connect up with the plots of the stories you were working. They seem highly integrated in *Tortuga* especially.

Anaya: I would hope that by *Tortuga* they would seem integrated, because it was my third novel and I had been consumed by that process long enough, and possibly also had learned a little bit about how to write a novel.

I have been told, when I travel around the country and read, that there haven't been that many American writers interested in the role of myth and in making myth work in contemporary settings—but I think now we see more and more writers doing that. All the Native American writers tend to do that, fuse their sense of myth into their stories, but at least for awhile it's been rather new to people.

The other thing that people seem to remark on is that not too many writers are lyrical novelists—you know, *Ultima* opens with a great deal of lyricism, a song of invocation almost, if not to the Muse then to the Earth, because Antonio says "In the beginning she opened my eyes and then I could see the beauty of my landscape, my llano, the river, the earth around us." There are other examples in American literature when that happens, but certainly it's been one of my preoccupations. I think the sense of diction and syntax and rhythms of language that come out of having grown up in a Spanish-speaking world, and the act of transferring that to English, creates a "fresh ripple" in people's sensibilities as they read this new language, this conversion of Hispanic language and world view into English. They may be a little shocked at the onset, but most people who get past it find it's refreshing, it's new.

Crawford: I was especially struck by the freshness of the language in the Christmas play scene in *Ultima* and when the children go to the theater in *Tortuga*— partly, I think, because these are scenes of rebellion against the norms of authority and partly because these are children in their spontaneity. There is such vitality in these scenes, where one set of cultural and social expectations crosses another. I suppose when you were writing *Ultima* there wasn't much like that in prose, even in Chicano prose.

Anaya: No, there wasn't—actually, I had read absolutely no Chicano prose during all my school years, including my university years. There were a few novels out there, and I suppose if you were into research you could have found diaries and newspapers, or in folklore you could have read the *cuentos,* but contemporary Chicano prose wasn't born until the mid-sixties during the Chicano movement, and so I think in a sense what we did in the sixties was to create the model itself, or as I have phrased it elsewhere, we set about to build a house and in the sixties we built a foundation. From that comes what we're seeing now in the eighties, an incredible amount of production and writing and unique forms and styles of writing. But all of that was new; it was new to me. In fact, in the sixties when I first began to work, I used Anglo American writers as role models. But I really couldn't get my act together until I left them behind. They had a lot to teach me and I don't underestimate that—you're learning whether you're reading a comic book or Hemingway or Shakespeare or Cervantes—but I couldn't tell my story in their terms. And it wasn't until I said to myself, let me shift for myself, let me go stand on my earth, coming out of my knowledge, and tell the story then and there—that's where Ultima came in. She opened my eyes as she opens Antonio's eyes at the beginning of the book, for the first time; so I sat down to write the story *Bless Me, Ultima,* thinking in Spanish though I wrote it in English. And it worked, because I was creating what to me was a reflection of that real universe that I knew was there.

Crawford: It seems tremendously integrated—not only as to myth and plot, as we were just discussing, but the style. I know you said you put it through several drafts; it looks as if it just sprang out of heaven that way. That must have taken an enormous amount of work.

Anaya: At least seven drafts *is* a lot of work. And then there is a concern for what you just said, that integration, that consistency that you don't want to give up in any one place, and a kind of conscious/subconscious working and interrelating of the myths and the symbols so that they all make a consistent pattern, like weaving a beautiful Navajo rug, you know? It's consistent because it reflects not only the particular person who does the weaving, but all the communal history that went into those symbols and those colors.

Crawford: There also you have the sense of the llano, probably best described there of the three books—and also the farming communities and the towns. And there's a juxtaposition of one against the other, shown in the conflicts of the two families. Was that from your own background? Were both sides of that conflict present within your own family?

Anaya: Yes, in fact, my mother is from a farming community and my father did most of his work as a *vaquero*—what you would call a cowboy or a sheep-herder—out on the llano in the ranches; so there was the antagonism between the *llaneros* and the farmers in my family.

Crawford: I love the way the farmers are people of few words. When they are talking to Antonio they will communicate in a few sentences what they have been thinking about all day. That seems to be true of farmers everywhere.

Anaya: Yeah, I think it is a characteristic, isn't it, of people who work with the earth to have imbued in them a sense of patience. On the other hand, they also have their own storytelling, and I remember visiting those farms along Puerto de Luna, where my grandfather had a farm, and late at night people would gather around and begin to tell stories. But the tradition was kind of different. The *llaneros* (*vaqueros* to me) would always be the loud men; they made a lot of noise, they were rough, they were gruff, they laughed more and probably drank more, so what you learned from the respective groups was very different, had its own flavor. . . .

Crawford: There's a strong sense in *Ultima* that the life experience cuts against some of the aspects of traditional Catholicism, so that there seems to be a sort of striving to supplant or transform it into a kind of world religion based on experience, especially mystical experience. Am I right about this? And did you encounter resistance from traditional Catholics for that message in the book?

Anaya: I've never felt there was any resistance or opposition. I think quite the contrary, a lot of readers who are Catholic have seen an accurate portrayal of the church at least as it was in those times—you're talking now about forty years later, and things have changed. But I think it's fair to say that what goes on in the novel also reflects my attempt to get an understanding of the Native American tradition and those other religions that are not Catholic and not based in the Christian mythology.

Crawford: Especially from the *indio.*

Anaya: Especially from the *indio.* And again, not to give up the one tradition for the other, but to see if those points of reference I talked about can be reached, whether from my Catholic world I knew as a child or my exploration of the Native American world that is also a part of me or the worlds that I read of in other mythologies, such as Buddhism. And so I think for me to look only in my Catholic background was too limiting, and *Bless Me, Ultima* begins to explore new ground.

Crawford: I was struck by the richness of choices that Antonio has at the end of the novel. He has many things to think about, reconcile, bring together.

Anaya: Well, his universe begins to get constricted. I think Antonio's life is—as he begins to see that he is losing the innocence of childhood—it possibly reflects the life of the Hispanic community in New Mexico, in the sense that we too began to lose that age when the only thing that affected us happened within our family or our village. The world was changing around us and was going to bring a lot of new and positive things to us, but also some threats. And we had a lot of decisions to make. Pretty quick.

Crawford: There's a thread of continuity in the books—literally, the same family is mentioned first in *Ultima,* is the whole subject of *Aztlan,* and the boy carries on in *Tortuga*—but also there is the thread of another kind of continuity. It seems to me that the three books are a trilogy, and in the third book is an overall interpretation you can bring—what the boy is going through personally somehow involves the whole culture, and his success, his survival, is a very important thing: an achievement for everyone.

Anaya: It's strange that no one has ever said that, you know. And I agree with your interpretation, because it seems to me that one of the important things I was doing in *Tortuga* was taking the main character and trying to make him well again after he had been crippled by life, by the circumstances that occur in *Heart of Aztlan*. And I felt that as much or more than any other character I had ever created, Tortuga was Everyman of the Chicano culture, that indeed the culture was under assault, and that the paralysis that had set on the community. Tortuga has not only to get well, he has to perform still more heroic tasks in the future; not only that, the Mexican American community has to find ways of breaking out of its bondage, its paralysis.

Crawford: It's also true that there are people from other cultures in the hospital who are also afflicted. . . .

Anaya: Yes, and in this respect I think the novel should acquire some kind of universal meaning, because what we have created of our modern society can paralyze all of us—those of us from minority groups get displaced more and used more, but I think if we are not careful the same forces that cripple us can do it to everyone. So you have in the hospital, even if they are never completely identified by ethnic group, representatives of all of them.

Crawford: In all three novels, the power of love is the redeemer in some sense. In *Tortuga* it's very much a literal one: It's sexual love, it's also working together—there's a wonderful sense of the people pulling together in a more collective spirit within the room he's in; there's real affection between the boys there—in fact, that seems to be the dominant message that your novels carry. . . .

Anaya: I think you're right. Though I have lived in and explored the existential universe, I have come back to a communal universe. I grew up in that tradition, I left it in some of my wanderings, and I returned to it; and what the tradition of the community has to teach us is what I've already alluded to—respect, love for the family and for the village that is the community. I think that's where the power of love comes in. I feel it has sustained all those Indian and Mexican pueblos that have occupied this region for such a long time; they must have had it as they came together and formed their bond—a bond not only of tradition and language and culture and heritage, but of love. That's how they were able to survive, and that's how they will be able to survive in the presence of all those powers that can cripple and kill us, you see.

Crawford: In *Heart of Aztlan* there is also that spirit of coming together, within the community established in Albuquerque, in the various parts of the barrio whatever the difficulty of the circumstances.

Anaya: One of the things that some critics have viewed as a failure in *Heart of Aztlan* has been that no structure, no political structure with a given political ideology, is put into place. But I guess my feeling is that while those structures may come into being, if they're not shored up by some common respect and a common goal that we have as human beings, they don't last long. And I do see their importance—they're the way we get things done in today's world. But I was more interested, I guess, in following the other side of that coin, and that is can we really get together as a community—not because of what's in it for me, but because of that old sense of value that has sustained all communities on earth throughout history. And to me, the element of love must play a large role in it.

Crawford: That brings me to a political question. You had clearly stated ten years ago that you didn't feel Chicano literature was strongest when it was narrowly addressed to political struggle and resistance. Ten years ago, the climate was very politically charged. What do you think about this now?

Anaya: What I have come to see is that there is even more need now for what we call a political stance, in our poetry and our novels. That seems to be a big change from where I was ten years ago. I guess I thought then that the literature we were writing would be very good for our community, one more place where we could reflect on our history and our identity and move on from there, and that we didn't have to overwhelm the reader with "message," so to speak; we didn't have to hit the reader over the head with ideology. I think that's principally the reason I wasn't in tune with the political writings of the Chicano movement at the time. I felt all too often that the ideology came up short—all too often it was only a Marxist ideology—and too, I tended to see in writers whose main concern was message a lack of aesthetic attention to what they were practicing, what they were learning to be. They didn't really want to be writers, they wanted to be politicians, and I think there's two different animals there. Can you get those two together in the same work? Can a very good writer who has learned and paid attention and practiced his craft communicate his political feelings about the society? I think yes; I feel stronger about that now than I did then. I still think it's probably the hardest kind of writing to do, because you tend to put the reader off. The reader wants story and you're talking message; the reader may quickly leave you. But it is important in this country, especially when you speak of our community, the Southwest. We have not only the story to write, we also have to remind our people about their history and their traditions and their culture and their language, things that are under that threat that we talked about right now, and liable to disappear if we don't look closely at ourselves in a historical process—and part of analyzing that historical process is not only story and myth and legend and tradition, it's a political space we occupy. How have we occupied it? How have we been used in that political space?

Recently I've played around with an essay in which I talk about writing in colonial space, which is a political concept, right? How do we feel as a minority group, a clearly recognizable ethnic group, when we have to respond to colonial space—how do we carve out our own identity? This is what the Chicano movement was all about, trying to create within colonial space the space for our own community, our literature. And that process is tied into the political process.

So in a sense you're always tied into it—I think my three novels are. The fact that they don't clearly call for one specific ideology may be interpreted as a critical fault in a political novel, but I didn't set out to write political novels. Though I do see their importance.

I think probably the novel that I'm writing now, which is again set in Albuquerque, is my analysis of my contemporary world, the present, today: What role do the different cultures of New Mexico play vis-á-vis each other? how is the Southwest changing? what is the concept of the Sunbelt all about? who is coming here and why are tremendous investments being made across the Southwest? what do they mean to our communities that have been here a long time? I think probably the only way we respond to some of these questions, critical questions if we're going to exist as a culture, *is* in novels that carry that social-political impact and perhaps allow the public to think on those questions that are crucial. But I'm still of the opinion that you do that through a well-told story.

Crawford: I've noticed there seem to be affinities between the ideas you're expressing and the writings of magic realism in Central and South America—being political in the broadest sense, describing what is happening in the Americas, and doing it with art—not leaving it to rhetoric. Do you have any direct relationships with Márquez or Fuentes or. . . .

Anaya: No, I haven't. If I were more inclined to go around visiting with writers, I would have found ways, but I'm not. I have one short story called "B. Traven Is Alive and Well in Cuernavaca" which begins something like this: "I don't go to Mexico to meet writers; I go to write!"

Crawford: I want to go back to *Tortuga*. It seems to me it's the most political novel you've done because it's the most concentrated on this extended metaphor we've been talking about—because that hospital is also a prison. The Indian boy that gets out dies very soon. It's as if people have been cut off from the land so that in going back to it, it becomes dangerous.

Anaya: Yeah . . . the idyllic and pastoral llano and river valley of *Bless Me, Ultima!* becomes the cancerous desert, the blinding sandstorms that you have to cross to get back home, the frozen mountain in midwinter that the Indian boy has to cross and that kills him. So even the land has almost become an antagonist, whereas before it was the nurturing mother. We get the sense of the unnatural storms, radiation, death in the desert, grasses described as brittle, and that's all part of the extended metaphor, the reflection of what we are doing to ourselves, what we are doing to our earth.

Crawford: One thing you did in that book struck me in a very personal way, because I spent some time myself in children's hospitals. It's where you talk about pain. You say that for someone who's had a great deal of pain, it's very hard to avoid things like drugs and alcohol later, because pain is a high and you get used to it. That's a very clear insight. When I read that I thought, "This guy has been there." You must have known something about that experience to be able to write that way.

Anaya: Yeah, well, I spent a summer in one of those hospitals and that's where the germ of the novel comes from—the experience, some of the characters, and some of the things that he went through. Around that is the reflection of what we are doing to ourselves and to the earth. It does have the hope in it that my characters seem to keep looking around—there must be *somebody* out there who I can make contact with—like the persons I knew in childhood who were a little wiser and more solid because they were sharing themselves. And even though the rest of the landscape alternates between the dead desert with the sandstorms and the frozen mountains around the hospital on the west side, the springs of the mountain are still running, there is still hope, it's not too late, and you can go there and you can bathe and be made whole. But there's very little of that left, you know. And we've got to touch base with it pretty quick. Otherwise, living in this region that has so much potential to it, because it's a very special corridor in this country, the Río Grande Valley and the cultures that have been here for thousands of years— it's a very special place—if we don't realize that, we're going to lose part of the hope that this region has to offer us and the people in it.

Crawford: We might end with one other question about that. It seems to me that some of the most responsible writers, as well as some of the best, from the three cultures here have written about this sense of place in one way or another—I'm thinking of Edward Abbey, who's really a westerner; Leslie Silko and Simon Ortiz; certainly yourself; and several others who have addressed it in a big way, in novels. What do you think the prospects are for this multicultural work becoming a national forum that people can begin to see as a model for such statements?

Anaya: I think that has already happened. I see any number of regions around the country that are in a sense turning inward and looking at themselves and producing wonderfully gifted writers. I'm not sure that we in the Southwest caused that forum; the times themselves are calling for a truly representative speaking to each other, letting down some of these false borders that we've had between us. I think that's a very positive thing. What's happening in this country—if we are part of it, much more power to us—is that if we are able to take our different perspectives of how the world ought to be—alerted to the fact that there are people out there who thrive on destroying—and share these perspectives, you know, communicate among groups, then we have something to offer the whole country and the world. The world *is* interested; that's one thing that is conveyed to me every time a visitor comes through here. They've locked into the Southwest as a place going through a very interesting experiment—it has to do with how people can live with each other, can share—and this is as important to the whites and the Maori of New Zealand as it may be to the Catalonians and the Basques, the Nicaraguans and the Misquitos, you know what I mean? It's important to us to realize that we are a center of focus—a lot of people are looking at us, and we can do something very positive with all the changes that are coming across this land, or we can blow it. And I tend to want to work more on the positive things that are going on here, so that we can learn from each other.

Interview with Rudolfo Anaya

Rubén Martínez / 1987

From *Writer's Forum*, 13 (Fall 1987): 14–29. Reprinted by permission of Rubén Martínez and publisher.

The following interview was conducted with Rudolfo Anaya at his Albuquerque home on February 20, 1987.

Martínez: There is a commonality in our experiences. I was raised in northern New Mexico in the fifties and we got our drinking water from a nearby spring or *ojo;* we heated our homes with woodburning stoves and lit them with kerosene lamps. Today, when I'm playing with computers and flying across the country in airplanes I feel like I am a traveler in time, traveling across the centuries. It is just an intuitive sense, but I am sure that you have the same feeling. I am wondering how this feeling has influenced your writings. Do you have the sense what I am talking about?

Anaya: Yes, I very much have the feeling that I have come from across cultures and through time, to use your phrase. But I think that most people have that feeling anyway. If you reflect on your life you become aware that life is a series of levels or times within the lifetime, and you simply outgrow a time and go to a new level. I think you can do that even if you remain in the same locality, the same town. In our case we obviously moved away from our small rural New Mexican towns, and we find ourselves caught up in the professional world that takes us, as you suggest, around the country to lecture. I think you cannot help but reflect on that; it is an interesting phenomenon.

Martínez: How has this feeling influenced your work? Where does this feeling enter?

Anaya: Well, I like the feeling because I like to travel. I have had the opportunity to travel. I have been to different places in the world. I like the feeling of moving to other worlds and other times, like being in Peru and Macchu Picchu, and in cities in China or even in villages in Greece. I have literally moved across time and space to view this world, then I come back

to my world and connect. I think that is a very refreshing thing to happen to
a person.

Martínez: Do you think that having had these experiences enhance your
capacity to relate to other cultures, to other peoples?

Anaya: Yes, absolutely. They not only enhance the capacity to relate to
people in their time and place but they give you a fuller understanding of
your own self. I am not only related to my rural New Mexican background,
I am related to the world, or I should be. There are a lot of rural towns all
over the world, as there are cities, as there are museums of art, and it is
interesting to make those connections and pull them together. I think it is
fulfilling to a person.

Martínez: As I was reading the short autobiographical piece that you sent
to me I recalled the speculation of others that your novels are based on personal experiences. I know that your novels transcend your personal experiences, but in this autobiographical statement you are very explicit about this
link, and people who read it will see that there really is a direct connection
to your novels. Can you say something about this connection?

Anaya: Well, I have always drawn from experience to create novels. When
I first published *Bless Me, Ultima* people asked me, "Is that you in *Bless Me,
Ultima?* Are you Antonio, the little seven-year-old character that starts the
novel?" My answer was always yes, you see, I have a very close relationship
to the characters I write about because they come out of my life. At the same
time you have to remember that fiction somehow transcends that reality, that
experience and reality that we use as a basis, as the ground, from which to
work. I then let it take off, let it spiral, let it create itself so that it is not a
completely historical reflection. I am doing it partially as a reflection of
where I come from, the people I came from, the towns I came from, the
barrio in Albuquerque here where I grew up, but always allowing the element
of the imagination to create fiction and to create art, to create some kind of
pattern out of that total experience.

Martínez: What is your understanding of art, whether it be literature,
painting, or music, and what is its role in the larger society?

Anaya: Well, for me art is that place where I go to think, to reflect on
myself. Whether it is music, or a painting, or a book or a poem it seems to
me that art is what connects me to the rest of the world, to humanity. It
teaches me that it is a reflection of my own nature and it does not matter who

does it, whether it is a Chicano writer or an African writer. In that sense it plays a very crucial role because that is one of the places, and there are other places, but that is one area where we can go to reflect. That reflection lets us know who we are and how we are growing or not growing, both as a communal group and as persons.

Martínez: The person and the group are linked dialectically?

Anaya: Yes. You also can add that the Chicano literature that we have been writing over the past twenty years begins to talk about the fundamental world view of the people, of the group. That is tremendously important. Again, you reflect on those values of that world view; without that reflection you, we are apt to be consumed by that which is not you, us, more easily. Part of the aesthetic values that we describe as beautiful, as valuable, also take place in art and in the constant experimentation that we call art or literature. So, I see its role as very crucial. I received a liberal arts education and am very grateful for it. At the same time I see its role, especially in our contemporary society, as a very crucial one.

Martínez: At this point in time specifically?

Anaya: Especially now, yes, because our society's orientation seems to be so grounded in material acquisition, in attention to strict science, and in attention to goals that have to do with values that are imposed from without. All of these things need to be constantly looked at by the individual and by the group that the person belongs to because all of those goals may not be worthy goals, and if you do not analyze them and reflect on them then you are apt to be sucked into believing that they are worthy goals.

Martínez: So, to some extent what you are saying is that art is a medium for the moral conscience of a group or a people?

Anaya: It is very true in our history that this is so because if you look at the *cuentos* that we grew up with and what the old people tried to inculcate in us you will find that they were teaching us literary history when they taught us our oral literary history. They were inculcating in us our world view, teaching us humor, and teaching us a sense of the aesthetic. Because they practiced their *cuentos,* they had devices that were techniques, and these were taught to us as well. So there was a great deal that was being taught to us, making us aware of our relationship to our community, to our family. Art is especially crucial to the Chicano population because if we do not look closely at ourselves we might—let me put it this way—the most blunt way to put it would be that we might be destroyed. That is, we might disappear if we do not pay strict attention to what is happening to us as a group. So, those of us who write not only continue the steps of our fathers, grandfathers, and ancestors, but we also have to use our literature in new and subversive ways so that our contemporary group, our contemporaries right now, come to us in the same sense that we went to our ancestors and reflect on the literature and what we are writing. They can therefore make clearer choices for the future.

Martínez: This subversion that you speak of, is it the subversion of this very broad process that characterizes a highly industrial and technological society? Is that what you refer to when you speak of subversion?

Anaya: Yes, that is part of it, but it also has to do with language, with history, with values. All of these things can be imposed from the outside on our community, and all of them may have some value. Because we live in a world that is multicultural and intercultural we live with many groups, that is a necessity. As I said before, it is kind of a refreshing world to live in when you see it in its multifaceted aspects. But it seems to me that there is a danger when particular groups within the multiplicity of cultures acquire too much power and instead of sharing important values they impose values. That becomes a problem that we have to address, and it should be addressed in art. So I think in that sense literature has to be subversive. It has to tell the community not only what has occurred historically but what is going on now.

Martínez: That brings two questions to mind. One is the perennial question regarding the relationship between politics and art, and the other has to do with the contemporary nativistic or anti-immigrant movement which seeks to make English the official language of the nation. This is also being done on a state-by-state basis. In *A Chicano in China* you wrote of the importance of language to group identity. Will you expound on that please?

Anaya: Well, I think the English Only Movement in this country is a reflection of fear. It seems to me maybe to get a little bit into your field of sociology, that when we have economic hard times or difficult times that have to do with war or when we perceive ourselves as being acted upon by aggressive outside forces, society seems to turn around with fear and looks at certain groups within it and attacks them as if somehow they are the cause or probable cause of that fear. I think that what we are seeing in our society is the mainstream society turning around and looking at the Spanish-speaking community in this country and saying, "You should all be speaking English because, if you do not, you somehow are tied up with all the problems that have to do with Latin America and immigration and so on." I see it as a people acting out of fear. Society breaks, it goes against the very grain of a pluralistic world, against the very grain of the sharing of languages, of acquiring more languages. It seeks instead to become a monolingual, monolithic nation.

Martínez: Ray Padilla, a specialist in bilingualism, sees language as a tool and a technology. His view is that denial of the opportunity to maintain our language involves technological loss and hampers our participation in the larger world.
Anaya: Absolutely. That's true.

Martínez: What about the politics question? I have read pieces where you have addressed this question, and other Chicano scholars also have addressed it. This subversion that you discussed earlier seems to place art in a very broad political arena. Do you perceive it in such a context?
Anaya: Well, I think that when we talk about what we write we are talking about an art form that really should touch all of life. Nobody writes a poem or a novel only to put it in a box labelled "Poem" or "Novel." We write to share with people, and our work should go out not only into the economic and political arenas, it should go to places where people are studying literature, religion, language, everything. I guess my definition of writing is that we are creating something that is very broad and should be available to the society at large in all its ramifications, not just one ramification.

Martínez: So that it would not be limited to one aspect of life?
Anaya: That's right. I think it is especially important for us who were writing during the Chicano Movement in the 60s and 70s to keep that broad and clear view about literature. I think part of the political problem within the Chicano Movement was that some of the critics or some of the leaders, say in the early Movement, expected only one type of literature. They expected a rhetorical message oriented vis-á-vis the Anglo-American society. We were suffering, we were oppressed, and we saw that very clearly in socioeconomic terms. So, there was a call to address only that issue. I simply could not see myself as a writer addressing only that issue. I was interested in a lot of other issues that had to do with who I am as a person and the community I come from.

Martínez: Do you think the decline in the intensity of the Movement created a context in which Chicano authors are freer to write?

Anaya: I don't know. The Movement, because of its intensity, was good. It was like we really had to look at ourselves and there was not much time. We had to know who we were as a people and where we were going as a community. A lot of that was very good. The intensity created a lot of poets, a lot of writers that would never have gotten going otherwise. On the other hand, I do notice now that we do not have the intensity of the late 60s and early 70s. Nevertheless, a lot of good writers and artists are coming about. So both times have something to contribute to the development of our art. I guess the only thing that I felt personally during the intense period of the Movement was the fact that some people, a very small group, wanted to be in charge of the message. To me, that was a limiting way to look at art.

Martínez: Was it the intensity of the Movement that helped you find your natural voice?

Anaya: No, I don't think so. In fact, to find your voice you really just have to trust your own instincts and write a lot. My voice comes principally out of the oral tradition of the *cuentos,* the stories that people used to tell, and just experimentation with my own techniques. I don't think that I have ever picked up a voice that tries to reflect a group movement. My voice is very personal, it is intimate, it's me. It has more to do with my upbringing as a child than anything else.

Martínez: So, your voice stems from your cultural background?

Anaya: It is the cultural background that I knew growing up in New Mexico, in Santa Rosa, in Puerto de Luna in the 40s and 50s.

Martínez: You have a personal voice, but also a group or communal voice. When I read your works, perhaps because I have a similar background, I can feel the tone, the message, at a level which is very personal to me and probably to all *manitos* in a very particular way, and to all Chicanos as well.

Anaya: Oh, see, that is what I am always striving for as a writer. I am trying to draw you, the reader, in as close as I can to what is going on in the story so that we can share it. That is exactly what the old people used to do when they told the *cuentos.* Listening to somebody tell a *cuento* we would be fascinated by the magic of the story, and possibly frightened if it was a scary story, but we were drawn into it. So that is what I strive to do. If there is a reflection of a communal voice in my work it is probably because each of us absorbs the values of our community and the interest our community has in storytelling. We reflect a bit of that in our writing.

Martínez: It also creates different levels of closeness between the readers and the characters in the story. For example, as a *manito* I feel a very intimate relationship with your characters and their experiences. I also know that art has broader, more universal messages so that people of other cultures can also relate to them. Generally speaking, would you say that Chicano literature and, more specifically, your works are understood by the community of Anglo-American literary scholars? If so, at what level of closeness is it understood?

Anaya: The levels of meaning that people respond to in any work of art should be universal. I should be able to read any writer in the world and respond to the world and the characters he creates because we are all human beings and we are all caught up in the same dilemmas. Cultures create colors, very interesting and fascinating colors, but at the root of the dilemma everything is human. The interesting thing about Chicano literature that you might be responding to is that on a level other than the universal the images presented in the novels and poems of our Chicano writers are specific. The images are specific images. Suddenly in *Bless Me, Ultima* you see Antonio. He is not a *gringito,* he is a *mexicanito* growing up here in New Mexico. The image is specific. He can be you, he can be someone like you or someone with whom you grew up. In the villages, we all knew people like *la curandera,* Ultima, the healers. So, the response is now not only universal, but it is closer to you, it's closer to all. Maybe, if nothing else when I said our literature has been subversive, the literature of the Chicano Movement, it was subversive because of this. We gave back to our community a specific image of itself. Members of the community could be close to it, they could be intimate, they could love or hate it, but at least it was them and they could recognize it as such. They recognized themselves in it.

Earlier you asked why I think art is important; it is because of this sense of reflection. You get into the story and you say, "Wow! This is me, or it could happen to me or this has happened to me." This sense of reflection is very important. What we are providing, those of us who write, is more immediacy to this reflection. If you read the novels being written now by Chicanas in the Southwest or anywhere in the country, you should be able to look at their image and say, "Good, now I understand myself better."

Martínez: How would you describe the present context of Chicano literature, and would you speculate as to its future?

Anaya: It is very open and very dynamic, very refreshing. A lot of Chicanas are producing now. I am writing a lot. So, I think the future looks very good, very bright. I am in touch now with young writers, students, people whose work I am editing. There is a lot of good work coming along. So, for whatever it is worth, whatever we did during the Movement, those of us who are already aged or coming out of the 60s and 70s, it is a good feeling because we can see that the social and political intensity may have died down a bit, but the artistic intensity has not, it has kept going.

Martínez: What about publishing outlets? You had trouble publishing your first major novel. Other Chicanos and Chicanas have had trouble publishing principally through the major publishing companies that are more accessible to other writers. Are we still forced to publish our own work?

Anaya: Yes. I think that of all the elements in the puzzle the hardest one to put in place is publication. It is fair to say that the major publishers in this country now are closed to Chicanos. We simply are not being accepted there. We have to continue to rely a lot on Chicano firms, Chicano publishers, and these are very limited. Right now there is more good quality work out there than is getting published. We have a lot of good work coming out that easily could be doubled or tripled if we had access to more publishing firms. So this is an extremely crucial problem.

Martínez: Let's turn to the topic of *la tierra.* How would you describe the *mexitos' connection to la tierra?* There is a relationship that is understood intuitively and cognitively, and your own world view seems to lend itself to understanding the intuitive relationship more than that of any of the other writers whose work I have read. Also, you write about the epiphany of landscape. How would you describe this relationship to *la tierra?*

Anaya: You are right. I have always seen it as deeply intuitive, probably even spiritual. The attachment that we have is, first of all, a long attachment. When you look at the Hispano Mexicano presence in New Mexico you see it dates back over 400 years. We have had time to really send our roots into the earth so that it cannot be anything except a spiritual connection. Because of our close relationship with the Native Americans along the Río Grande and because of our very own nature, our own heritage as native Americans, we also have that connection with the earth. You take these two elements and what you have is a communal group that for a long period of time relied on the earth for subsistence, thereby becoming very tied to the cycles of weather, of planting, of nurturing, of watering, of caring. It is easy to see why the

tierra becomes *la madre tierra.* The Native American concept of mother
earth is one that is very close to us.

Martínez: Some critics have stated that your work harkens back in sadness
and nostalgia to a forgotten, idealized, and unattainable past. Do you think
this is a fair criticism of your work?

Anaya: Yes, sure. Anything is fair criticism so long as it is done right. It
seems to me that there are a lot of ways by which we can define Chicano
literature, and one of the definitions comes out of the continuing dialectic
between us, as Chicanos, and the mainstream Anglo American culture. That
culture imposed itself on our land in the mid-nineteenth century, after the
war with Mexico. One view of Chicano literature, then, would be that it must
always reflect this continuing problem. I have no argument with this view. I
think it is crucial and important for our understanding of who we are as a
community. I mean it is history, and it is there. We see everywhere around
us the outcome of that historical process, right? So I see it and I understand
it. But, another way to understand ourselves is to look at our world view, that
is, our soul. Looking at how we were formed and where we come from leads
me to give as much importance or, perhaps, more importance to relationships
such as the one we have with *la tierra.* I just cannot take these 400 years or
more of my history or heritage and say that they no longer mean anything—
they do. Even though I now live in a city, I'm an urban dweller, I still see
this relationship that we have had historically as being of prime importance
because out of that relationship come all the other relationships; the relationship with the community, what we do together, how we were taught to live
together, relationships of harmony to people, to community, to earth. I just
do not want to throw these out the window. They are not what nurture me
but what inspire me. My dreams come out of there, why should I toss them
out the window? Even in the city we can still have our *jardincitos* [small
gardens]. Those of us who have that love for the land, we have to keep working it.

Martínez: So you would not say then that there is a longing for the past,
rather there is a sense that knowing our past helps us to understand ourselves
today.

Anaya: If by longing for the past you mean a desire to return to the past,
then I have to say that I know that I cannot return to the past of my childhood
or the past that my grandfather knew, say in Puerto de Luna as a rancher, as
a farmer, and as a complete communal man. But that past does not have to

be dead. I carry it in my memory. I write about it and I think it is a very useful element, it is just part of me. So I am not longing to return to a specific time, I am just exploring what went on in that history, exploring those relationships and their importance, and letting them become part of the soul of the story.

Martínez: You have mentioned the collective unconscious in at least one of your pieces. Tell me how you understand it.

Anaya: I understand it to mean that somehow we are all connected. I understand myself as belonging to what I call a community or a tribal group. I am a member of a tribe. I not only have a personal history and a personal memory, but that group also has a group memory. I find it very fascinating to try to tap into that group memory through myself and come up with the symbols, the resources, the values, dreams, relationships, and the way of looking at the world that are not only particular to me but are particular to my tribe. That is how I understand the collective memory.

Martínez: There also is in your works a search for harmony in the universe, at least I detect it. I do not know if you have even been explicit about it, but can you relate to me your understanding of this search for harmony?

Anaya: Essentially, I think that is what all of us want to have inside, a certain peace of mind, a certain harmonious relationship to our fellow human beings and to the universe. We want to understand why we are here and what our purpose is in life. A great deal of my searching for harmony seems to come out of Native American thought, Native American religious thought. It comes out of their concepts, their ideas of how you create harmony in your community, how you relate to God, if you call it God or if you call it *kachinas,* and how you relate to the elements of nature. They have to do with how you relate the subsistence of the pueblo to rain and snow, or the lack of them. I feel very tied to the natural world, to the natural elements, and to the harmony that exists there. When I see that harmony and I reflect on it I have a desire to be harmonious with it and within myself. So, I think it is a process of life where a person searches for its meaning. The meaning in life to me is not to acquire position or wealth, it is to achieve harmony within myself.

Martínez: Have you studied Native American religions and cosmologies or is it an intuitive understanding that you have?

Anaya: I have never done what I would call a strict academic study of Native American religions or cosmologies. I pick up a book here and there. I am very much the type of person that likes the intuitive approach. It's what I learn when I meet people or when I am at the pueblo, at a dance, or when someone gives me an article or a book. I like to run into the experience or find it within myself, that is more my approach.

Martínez: There is one short story of yours which is quite different from all the others, although one certainly can find similarities in the universal meaning of your work. The story is "The Captain." What prompted you to write this story and why a Nazi officer?

Anaya: Oh, that is a . . . I was going to say that's a strange story, and all stories are strange in how they come. That story was a dream. I saw the images in a dream. I got up in the morning and I came to my study and wrote it. Principally, I think it is about perversion. In this case Hitler, who has so much power, falls into perversion, and power, to get back to harmony, acts against harmony. So, I just wrote it. The dream was so vivid, I don't know why it came to me.

Martínez: Have you reflected on why you had the dream?

Anaya: No. There was no tie to anything that had happened right before I had it. I had not seen a movie or read a book. I was not thinking about the Nazi era in Germany at all. The dream came that night. The image was vivid enough for me to get up and write the story, and that's it.

Martínez: Have you had any responses to the story?

Anaya: Well, it is in a little anthology that few people have looked at, so I have not had very many responses. It has not been widely circulated.

Martínez: Let's talk about your major works. Most of your critics seem to agree that *Bless Me, Ultima* is your best novel and that those that followed it were not of the same quality. Yet in your autobiographical statement you wrote that *Tortuga* is your best work. Will you tell me why you say this?

Anaya: *Bless Me, Ultima,* I think, has several things going for it. Number one, it is a first novel and writers who are lucky with their first novel tend to get tagged with them a great deal. Quite frankly, without being immodest, I think it captures the soul of part of our community. So, people responded to it. This gets back to that image and people reflecting on it.

When *Heart of Aztlan* came out I think people were expecting a second installment of *Bless Me, Ultima* and were disappointed. By the time I got to *Torgua* I had learned many of the techniques of writing. I had progressed. I was exploring a different universe but I was still dealing with the natural elements, water, the mountain, and so on. There also is mythic content. Readers who read *Tortuga* carefully, and who are, say, judicious readers, have the same response I have. They like it. They really like it once they get into it, but it is not an easy novel to read, there is a lot of suffering in it. It is not the kind of thing you pick up to read in bed.

As for the critics, I cannot comment very much on how the public or the critics respond to my novels. My goal in life has been to keep writing, and I have tried to write in as many forms as I can. I have written short stories, novels, and plays. I have a children's story I am going to publish this year. I have several essays. I even wrote one epic poem, *The Adventures of Juan Chicaspatas.* I am very interested in all sorts of writing and forms and find it a challenge to experiment in these forms. My intent is just to keep writing and not worry if one of my works is liked more than another.

Martínez: What inspired you to write the epic poem and what would you say is its essential meaning?

Anaya: The epic poem requires a long explanation because *The Adventures of Juan Chicaspatas* is a section in a new novel I am writing. It takes place in a scene when the writer is called upon to recite the poem, so he recites it. This happens a lot in bars. In fact, the scene takes place in a bar where a bunch of people are gathered to talk and drink. One of them is asked to recite the poem, he recites it, then later the characters in the poem become characters in the novel. Do you see now why the explanation is very long?

I took the epic poem out since it was complete and it got published by itself, which is fine. Its meaning is the meaning that I have had since I began writing. It has to do with Juan Chicaspatas and Al Penco, his friend, going back to Mexico, to Aztlán, to the meaning of this New World. We will find the definition of the New World Man by going back into our history, by going back into our collective memory, to use that term, and by going back to our values. The New World person, that is who I want to be and that is what I am after. I will more closely understand that New World Man by understanding my indigenous history. So, they go back and understand part of the legends of their original homeland, which doesn't have to be Aztlán, it could be Taos. Somewhere we have that sense of our original homeland, our original values, our communal values, and we have to understand them. I think one of the crucial questions we have to face is how Chicanos have been cut off from that understanding historically. The educational system has not given it to us and that is why we are a dispersed people. We are not completely in touch with our own history and that has been one of my purposes in writing, to bring that understanding back to my community.

Martínez: One of the features of Chicano literature is a search for identity, perhaps a search for an understanding of our role in the universe. Would you say, then, that this poem is in this genre?

Anaya: Yes, there is a search for identity and for our homeland. These are brought back because, as you know, the poem ends with them saying, "Now we have to go out into the world and teach everybody what we saw on our return to the indigenous world."

Martínez: Let's talk about your trip to China. The tone of the journal is exhilarating. It sounds like you and Patricia and the others were really excited about your experiences. Your excitement comes through in your journal. Are there some themes that you have had time to reflect on that were not included in the journal that you would like to expound upon now?

Anaya: Themes that were not included that I would have loved to have put in? There are too many to mention. I look back and think of all the tofu we ate, and I think I do not mention it even once in the journal. Yet, there is such a thing as tofu. I could go on and on. Almost everyday I meet people who have gone to China or are going there, and just in brief conversations people mention this or that.

This morning before you arrived my wife and I were talking about Shanghai, one of the last cities we visited. We were talking about how over crowded it is with the new apartments that are being built, about the lack of heating in the apartments, and about the city being rundown. There are realities that I wanted to talk about that come up now and I say, "Gee, I wish I had gotten those in the journal." It's too late, you see. I had so much time each night to write and my impressions were very personal, you know, what I had done, what they had caused me to think, and so on. Maybe I will have to wait for *A Chicano Returns to China* to get in the rest.

Martínez: One of the things captured beautifully in the journal is your personal touch. You communicate at a personal level with your readers, and you explicitly state that you wanted to share your experience with the community.

Anaya: Yes. When I started writing the journal, I felt I had to talk to someone. So, while I was writing my entries at night I would talk to *la Raza* back in New Mexico, and say, "*Raza,* if you could just be here with me now, here is what you would see, here is what I am feeling, and here are the connections I'm making.

Martínez: That comes through in the journal because as I was reading it I could really connect with some of the similarities you saw between the familiar here and the foreign over there. I was saying to myself that *manitos* were going to connect with the journal, and had they been there with you they would have made similar comparisons between the familiar and the foreign.

Anaya: Well, as I state in the journal, I have been very fortunate to be able to travel and one of the things that is important in the education of our young is to have that same opportunity and the same excitement about seeing the world. We are a very important communal group in the context of world groups and the more we know about all those other communities the better it will be for our people, our group. So, I have that desire to get these Chicanitos going to China, to Tibet, and to every corner of the world. I admire nations that do that with their young people. They send them out and expose them to other people from all over the world. I think we have to do more of that.

Martínez: On your trip to China you seem to have been more fascinated by dragons than by the golden carp. I believe that your readers would not have expected this.

Anaya: Well, you see, the dragon was very interesting in 1984 because I had already begun work on my novel which will be published this year. It is called *Lord of the Dawn,* and it is my retelling of the legend of Quetzalcóatl, the Toltec diety that is part dragon and part bird, the plumed serpent. So, perhaps that energy of the Chinese dragon was calling to me because I was involved with the Toltec, indigenous Native American dragon. That is the only way I can explain it. It was very fascinating to be working on that novel, to have it in the back of my head, and at the same time be hit with the reality of the Chinese dragon and what it means. If the Asiatic continent sent emigrants to the Americas, then the largest number of Americans are originally an asiatic people. Talking again of the collective memory, we can ask what they brought with them. Is Quetzalcóatl a distant dream or memory of the original Chinese dragon, and what are the aspects that define that dragon?

Martínez: You went there seeking connections between Meso-American cosmologies and the ancient civilizations of China. You probably cannot make those connections in the sense that sociologists would like to see them made, that is empirically, but you undoubtedly made intuitive connections. Would you relate those connections?

Anaya: Well, from my point of view I insist that I can make those connections, and I do not care to make them as a scientist. I think the connections I make are the ones that are in the journal, connecting the dragon and its energy, connecting the golden fish, which is an asiatic fish, to my childhood at Santa Rosa. I connected dreams I had in China with New Mexico, and I connected persons who visit me in my dreams to myself. What is the power of dream? I do not know. They all seem to fit in China because the place was so foreign and so far way, so distant, yet it reminded me that the world is not that big. The world is small.

The best feelings were in the communes where the farmers were at. I had this definite feeling that my grandfather, who was a farmer, could have sat and talked with those men without any problem at all, without the politics of the world getting in the way.

Martínez: Did you find harmony?

Anaya: Finally, yes. At the end I think I did. It was not there at the beginning. It was a very threatening trip at the beginning, but I guess I should say I began to find it. I began to pull it together and have a clear understanding of why I went there and what happened to me there.

Martínez: The journal ends with a postscript which conveyed a sense of uneasiness, a sense of distress or perhaps, at another level, harmony. What are you communicating in the postscript?

Anaya: Well, I think that is the thing about going to a different world, about traveling. If we are really wise we will open ourselves up to the experience, become like sponges and take in everything. Well, that is a frightening thing. You see, by taking in everything you can change beyond what you had planned. You leave yourself open to experience. Not very many people do this and yet that is exactly what I am suggesting we have to do. So, I felt that I had opened myself up and I had taken the Chinese people, their dragon, parts of their religion, their cities, and everything into myself. And yes, for awhile it was not going to be harmonious. I had taken in too much too soon. I had to come back to my earth and settle myself. Working on the notes of the journal when I came back really helped me put it in perspective.

Rudolfo Anaya

Feroza Jussawalla / 1992

From *Interviews with Writers of the Post-Colonial World,* eds. Feroza Jussawalla and Reed Way Dasenbrock. University Press of Mississippi, 1992, 245–55. Reprinted by permission of publisher.

Rudolfo Anaya is the Chicano writer who has—with Rolando Hinojosa—created the most substantial oeuvre. Born in 1937, he is the author of three novels, including the best known Chicano novel, *Bless Me, Ultima,* and a book of short stories. But he has also written plays, children's stories, a travel book, *A Chicano in China,* has edited a volume of essays and two collections of stories. He is a true man of letters and has also worked hard to encourage other Chicano and southwestern writers to develop their own voices. The following interview was taped on a visit by Anaya to El Paso (and then followed up on at his home in Albuquerque), where true to this sense of responsibility, Anaya visited with students, taught a class and did a reading of his fiction.

Feroza Jussawalla: I've used *A Chicano in China* a lot in my classes because it speaks to my students, here in El Paso, about identity and crossing cultures. In a way you've made identity the central issue in the book. In what ways does China speak to you? There's quite a bit of reference in *A Chicano in China* about the connection between the Chicanos and the Asians. Your grandfather, for example, puts his ear to the ground, and he says that you can hear the Chinese. You have a whole theory about Asian immigration from Asia through the Northwest coast into the Llano area, into New Mexico, establishing a connection between the Chinese people and the Chicano people. I'm interested in this partially because I'm from Asia and I'm living in New Mexico. How did China and Asia become relevant to your personal history?

Anaya: I have always been very interested in the migrations of people, especially in the Southwest. This has been a migration path since time immemorial. Basically, the migrations from the Asiatic continent took place from North to South. Those people came across the Bering Strait and then settled all of the Americas and kept going to Tierra Del Fuego. That's a very important migration. If you look at the legends of the Aztecs, they talk of that

migration. We came from north of Mexico; we came from Aztlán. That was
one of their stopping places in their migration. Then you get the migration of
the Español going in the opposite direction, going upstream from Mexico up
into Nuevo Mexico. Then finally in the last century you get a new migration
of the Anglo-American coming East to West and running into this very important corridor. What happens in these corridors of migration interests me—
how people treat them, how they live there, what consciousness and new
awarenesses they come to and what kinds of conflict develop when different
peoples mix, as we have here in the Southwest. We have the Indio, Español,
Mexicano, and finally the Anglo-American. I use the metaphor of being a
fish in the stream of migration—which I think blends perfectly into the
golden carp and the fish people that I have always used as a theme in my
work. So here I was swimming upstream of the original migration, thinking
of that part of me that is native American, that is, what I call the New World
man, and feeling very much at home because by going to China I had returned to part of my roots, my symbols, and the Sipapu, the homeland. Aztlán
might be in China, if you push it back far enough, if you push it back to its
original source. I have always traveled and tried to see what I have in common
with people, how we all fit into the human salad. It was very natural for me
to see myself as a Chicano Chinaman. I became a Chicano Chinaman.

F.J.: Is this a revelation that came to you upon going to China, or had you
always thought about this?

Anaya: No, everything evolved naturally. I didn't preplan anything or plot
anything. I went with an open mind. The allusions to my grandfather were
very important because I've always used a mentor or a guide for my characters in my literature. I felt the need, especially in this trip, to have a mentor,
a guide. The place was very foreign, very far away, very strange, and I really
knew it only through the stereotypes that we most often have of foreign
countries, especially of the East. I alluded to this in the work, to Charlie Chan
movies; what else did we know about China? So I was trying to learn the
truth about China, not the stereotype, and I felt someone like my grandfather,
a wise old person, would be that spiritual guide that I needed, that mentor.

F.J.: Had he any connection with China or Asia?

Anaya: This man lived all his life in a little valley in New Mexico, in the
Puerto de Luna valley. He was a farmer, he was born there, he was raised
there. The old people didn't know a world beyond that, but they were so
intuitively wise enough to know that we are connected to the world out there.

F.J.: You've said before that when you're asked about your roots, you look down at your feet, and there your roots are, and that's just New Mexico. So your roots lie in New Mexico rather than tracing any Spanish genealogy? How do you see yourself in that context?

Anaya: My roots are in New Mexico because New Mexico is one of the Indo-Hispano cultures of the New World. What I am trying to do in my work and when I talk to people, is—by having them look down at their feet and their roots, at the soil of the New World—to take a meaning and identification from it. We don't have to go to Europe or to Spain to find our roots. We have finally become New World persons. I think if we don't do that, we will never meet our authentic selves. We'll always be rushing to Spain as the mother country. Those connections are important, those roots are there, but we have evolved in the New World.

F.J.: Can you give me your definition of the New World man? What does he incorporate?

Anaya: The New World man, the New World person, takes his perspective from indigenous history and spiritual thought and mythology and relationships. The New World person is a person of synthesis, a person who is able to draw, in our case, on our Spanish roots and our native indigenous roots and become a new person, become that Mestizo with a unique perspective. That's who we are and how we define ourselves.

F.J.: That tension is played out very strongly in *Bless Me, Ultima* because you have the Lunas who identify with the Spanish colonizers and who cultivated the valley and grew things and made it green, and then you have the Marez, the vaqueros, the people of the Llano. How did you come to working that tension out?

Anaya: As I look back in my work, as I said in the essay "The New World Man," which I read at the conference in Barcelona this past summer, it seems to me I have always been in search of this person. I have not been able to feel authentic until I found this person because I was being led to believe I was too many other things by too many foreign, outside influences that I didn't even know who I was. So how could they describe me? Looking back at *Bless Me, Ultima,* at least one way to describe Antonio is that Antonio is the beginning of my search for the New World person. He incorporates the Español and the Indio, the old world and the new.

F.J.: I've used chapter six of *Bless Me, Ultima* in my freshman classes a great deal. That's the chapter in which Antonio comes to school for the first time. The teacher looks at him and calls him Tony, and then the students make fun of him when he's eating his lunch of tacos. It's an experience that must speak out to my students because my students respond: "Oh yes, this happened to me, this happened to me," and they respond to it with a genuine gut feeling. Is that a colonization process you're depicting, a new colonization, the way in which someone like Antonio is colonized into becoming an American?

Anaya: Yes, but after all, this area that I speak about and this corridor that I belong to, this Río Grande spiritual corridor, has always been colonized. There have been successive colonizations, successive migrations. People pass through and make this place their home. When the Anglo-American finally comes here in the mid-nineteenth century, he becomes the most recent colonizer of the indigenous peoples, and so Antonio in that chapter, and I think probably in all of the book, reflects that indigenous person. I think a lot of people have missed this in the book, but my concern is how will Antonio ever find himself, truly see himself?

F.J.: Can you tell me how he will?

Anaya: It's going to be a long process because the reality of the colonization mode or model is to destroy the roots that bind you to the authentic self. Everybody has to search, to continue searching. It happened to my generation, and you're saying your students still reflect on that; so it's still happening. I believe that history and literature and all the arts are important; they feed the person that we really are because they go to our values and our roots.

F.J.: I've talked about *Bless Me, Ultima* with Rolando Hinojosa, and he said that most people consider *Bless Me, Ultima* as a mythical novel, but that it is really a political statement. Do you see a political statement in *Bless Me, Ultima,* and if so what would you say it is?

Anaya: I've just told you that the novel has a structure by which a boy who is very small begins to inquire into who he really is. When you find who you really are, you become a person of incredible power.

F.J.: What I was thinking of was the scene when he finally decides he's not going to become a priest, or does he decide that?

Anaya: I would hope that he would be a shaman, but, you know, a shaman is another kind of priest. The point is not so much what he becomes. We can't dictate what people become, but what we can hope to do is to liberate people by having them become their most true selves, their authentic selves, to find their deepest potential. Then you will recognize the models of colonialism that are set over you, and you'll know how to react and how to accomplish your goals in life. So to me the important aspect of *Bless Me, Ultima* is that process of liberation.

F.J.: Antonio is essentially shucking off two levels of colonialism—one is the Spanish colonialism that comes through his mother's family, the religious colonialism of the Catholic church, and at the same time the kind of Anglo-American colonialism that's coming to him through the Anglo-American education system.

Anaya: I think that's fair to say.

F.J.: What about the people of the Golden Carp? Do they ever get set free, or do they just go around in a circle?

Anaya: I'm not sure I follow that line of thinking.

F.J.: Antonio says at one point that the Golden Carp is never set free from Narciso's mythology. He says it's never set free, it just goes around and around seasonally.

Anaya: You must know that in one sense no one is ever set free. This is the nature of our humanity. We struggle to be free, and we struggle depending on the philosophy that we follow, right? If I wish to achieve a total freedom, must I die, or must I turn to the Zen or to Nirvana or to the Buddha or become a priest for the Catholic church? I don't prescribe and tell people what will set them free, but I'm very interested in the process. There is a process by which you can get to know yourself and to be liberated in yourself. That liberation also has a very important component in the community because as you liberate yourself, you liberate others, and you get to know more of your humanity. I am interested in that process; other people will be interested in the political ends of that process.

Culture is something we create. We're creators of culture; we love it, you know. And in many ways, there is as much of a trap there as in anything else. I'm interested not only in the individual, but in the communal group. I'm also interested in the fact that cultures can be as binding and enslaving as anything else. But they can also provide the context where you explore your relationships with other people, explore the possibility of being that authentic self I talk about. So nothing is good or bad categorically; it's what we make it. I think that we have the possibility of making our culture a vehicle for the exploration of that self, for communal fulfillment. Perhaps I'm being too idealistic, but I really believe that is possible in community because that's all we have. We look around and we only have each other, and how we relate to each other is important.

F.J.: So the "Heart of Aztlán" doesn't have any kind of particular specific locus for you. It shifts with communities and people, would you say?

Anaya: No, I think it has a definite locus. It is a Barrio which is a definition of community, set in a specific place and a specific time with specific goals.

F.J.: I don't mean the novel with that title, *Heart of Aztlan,* as much as metaphorically. Does the culture have a specific locus or can it move to communities and cultures in Northern New Mexico or Southern New Mexico or West Texas?

Anaya: Everything we write should be able to move like that. Everything we write should be able to move out into the world and be a reflection of everybody else's community.

F.J.: I don't know how you'll receive this question, but is that why you write in English? I'm beginning to get more and more feedback from writers who say, "oh to be authentically Hispanic, we should be writing in Spanish, or to be authentically African, we should be writing in an African language, or to be authentically Indian we have to write in an Indian language." Does your sense that writing should speak to everybody govern your choice of language?

Anaya: I didn't have a choice. I was educated in the American school system, and this school system teaches English. So very quickly I moved from my native tongue, which is Spanish, into the English language both spoken and written. So the choice was not there to make. By the time I started writing I was a university student, I'd been fourteen years in the English-speaking world and English-writing world. What choice did I have?

F.J.: If you had the choice, would you have chosen Spanish? Or is English part of the New World man's consciousness?

Anaya: No, the New World man's consciousness is language free; he can use any language to express it.

F.J.: So there are really no considerations of audience. It's just that the language that comes naturally to you as you write is English.

Anaya: Yes, by now it comes more naturally of course. I think that in terms of language one does what one can do best with one's resources. I didn't pursue a study of Spanish. The Chicano writers who are part of the Chicano movement generation who took degrees in Spanish-language departments wrote in Spanish. It's easy for those who write in Spanish to use that as a political statement. I try to be more realistic, I deal with reality. I was brought up and educated in this language so I use it, and I didn't think about audience when I started writing in English. It was just that by that time I had been trained and gotten my degree in an English department, so that was natural.

F.J.: One thing that's very natural in your writing style is the way in which you switch back and forth between Spanish and English.

Anaya: I think we're all, in many ways, multilingual people. Most of us Chicanos in the Southwest are surely bilingual. So it comes naturally sometimes to shift back and forth. But it is more important to use rhythms of Spanish in our work, the rhythms of Spanish in the Southwest, which is a unique blend of Spanish.

F.J.: But then in the *Cuentos* anthology of traditional stories or tales from New Mexico that you've edited you've worked consciously at having one page in Spanish and one page in English.

Anaya: That was an editorial decision. My friend had done the collection in Spanish and he said: "I want to present a book bilingually; will you do the English translation?" and I said yes.

F.J.: Do you think that many Chicano writers feel compelled to succumb to that pressure of having to include Spanish, even though they may have, like you, grown up mastering the English language initially?

Anaya: They might. The only problem with writers who throw in Spanish for effect is that it sticks out like a sore thumb; you see it right away. My advice would be to write with the tools you have, what you can compose in well. The craft of writing anything is difficult enough as it is.

F.J.: Is there a publication problem with using Spanish and English, moving back and forth?

Anaya: Absolutely. In this country, you cannot get works written in Spanish published. It's difficult. There are very few publishers who touch manuscripts written in Spanish. Then it would be difficult to market and distribute them.

F.J.: One of the things that interests me a great deal in your work is just the way in which you focus on the individual and bring out the individual, and then you bring the mythology in, like you did in the story you read yesterday about the desert and the dust in the mouth. How does all that come together for a writer? How do you mix the mythology with individual characters?

Anaya: I have been in training all my life to be this person, to be this writer. I am aware of a goal that I have set in life that I want to accomplish, and I work at it.

F.J.: Is it knowledge of myth together with knowledge of human psychology and observation, or is it mostly observation of individuals?

Anaya: It's a knowledge, but more than knowledge it's an exploration into what makes us human, the human soul, the human condition, intuition. I don't study mythology. I read myths; I'm interested in mythology, but that's not a real study I have. Myths are personal; they come from your dreams and your subconscious. We all have them, and we all have the ability to know each other, and I'm more interested in what drives us. I'm interested in passion and desire and how all these show up in different forms in mythology.

F.J.: There's a very close tie-in between landscape and human beings in your work. Does the landscape make people be a certain way?

Anaya: Absolutely, yes. If you begin to go back to mythology, one statement, one phrase I have used, and I don't know if I made it up or I read it somewhere, is, "The gods come from the landscape." The gods come from the sea and the trees and the mountains and the caves and the forests, and people responding to those landscapes are responding to those gods. By responding to the gods you're responding to the landscapes. Different landscapes give rise to a different form of gods and demons.

F.J.: In your more recent work, you are moving gently off the Llano into the desert. You're not really moving into the Río Grande Valley, but off into the desert.

Anaya: No, I'm moving into the city.

F.J.: In your new work? Can you talk about that?

Anaya: Well, look around and make a list of every writer in the Southwest. Ninety percent or more of them live in cities, and this has been true since World War II, since the migrations began from the Llano and the desert and the villages and small towns into the cities! So now we have to deal with urban landscapes, or we should be dealing with them. The writers of the

Southwest and the West resist dealing with that urban experience, but it is who we are; it is us.

F.J.: That's because the landscape has been romanticized in Western and Southwestern literature in a certain kind of way, and that's kind of a colonial factor too. When we talk about Third World literature, we talk about the colonial literature, about the area or about the landscape: E. M. Forster about India's landscape versus the Indian writers about India. Is it perhaps this romanticizing of the landscape that makes a writer a Southwestern writer?

Anaya: I don't know if the landscape and how we use it would be a criteria for definition. I tend to think it is. In reading through anthologies and books of these Southwest writers who live in cities, they constantly place their stories back in the old Rancho, or the little village, or on the highway, or in the cafe in the outskirts of town. It's just something in us to do that. We are part of the myth, and we perpetuate it, you know?

It's good and bad like everything else, right? It can be made to work for you and it can also become a formula that's not very interesting after a while. I've been in the city most of my life, so I can't continue to write *Bless Me, Ultima* of the small town. I am no longer that. I must confront my new landscape which is an urban landscape.

F.J.: And in what ways do you confront that?

Anaya: By writing about it, by using it as the backdrop, by studying the dynamics of the Southwest city, the new migrations that are coming here, the new models of colonialism. How are the new migrations of the last ten or twenty years into the Sunbelt changing our cultures, our traditional cultures? Who's in charge now? Who's suffering? All of that is taking place in the city.

F.J.: Is this a new phase of the diaspora experience in that the Mexican-Americans are becoming part of the larger diaspora, or becoming part of the mainstream? What exactly is it about the urban landscape that engages you?

Anaya: The fact that we live in it. Everything about it should engage us. I don't know if dealing with the urban landscape is a return from the diaspora or not. I don't know if the barrio can any more be the focus of our community. The Chicano is entering the mainstream, the middle class. There is no doubt about that. There are people who will argue it, but by and large, that's the drive. And it brings up one more cycle of our history. We are wrapped up as part of the human condition in cycles. The important thing, I think, is to look at this new cycle. What are we like now that we enter the urban landscape, professional jobs, middle-class mainstream? To use your comparison, what will Antonio's role be today? If he had stayed in Ultima's Llano, he would be the new shaman. I think there's a job for him to do in Albuquerque, New Mexico, or in El Paso, where people still need literature to reflect on their condition. That's what literature does.

F.J.: What is the job for educators in this new urban landscape when we come across our Hispanic-American students? Is it to bring out their Hispanicity more or to make them mainstreamed? Is it to encourage their use of Spanish versus their use of English, or to get them to use both? Is it to rouse a sense of the colonized individual in them?

Anaya: I think our role as educators is to give them a real grounding in what we call the humanities, to help them read the classics and good literature and world literature and the literature of their group—to read the Chicano writers. If we are *not* to become the new colonizers, our role is to set them free. That's always been the role of the teacher. So I don't see that that role has changed; in fact, it's more crucial now than ever because the American popular culture has such a grip on young people. It inculcates them with a world view and a system of values that is so empty and void and has so little meaning that we are poised at a perfect point in history in terms of telling young people look, there is good literature—read it, there is history—read it, reflect on it, find yourselves and go out and do something good for mankind, for people.

F.J.: What classics would you have them read?

Anaya: World classics from all cultures of the world. If you're talking about Hispanics students now, Chicano students, I would say that would include a lot of the mythology and the classical thought of indigenous, pre-Hispanic America. Also read the contemporary Chicano writers, but read them always with a sense of fulfilling yourself.

F.J.: What tradition do you see yourself writing in, or what tradition would you like to see yourself in? I guess I want to make this a two-part question. What have been the literary influences on you, and what tradition do you see yourself in? Did the influences on you come from American literature, British literature, or indigenous Hispanic literature, or indigenous Native American literature? And should the Chicano writers be seen as part of a stream of American literature?

Anaya: I think the influences came from all of those sources, including some of what I call the world classics. I consider myself very much a Chicano writer, but I think eventually we will be one more voice in that make-up of what is the literature of the United States. Eventually, I would like to see that what I have written and what I am writing is a search for a unique person, a person that has not been written about very much in the literature of the United States, and a person that is not known in this country. There is this New World person, essentially he is a mestizo, he is myself and that's what I've been exploring in my writing.

Interview with Rudolfo Anaya

R. S. Sharma / 1992

Reprinted from the *Prairie Schooner,* 68.4(1994): 177–87. By permission of the University of Nebraska Press and R. S. Sharma. Copyright 1994 University of Nebraska Press.

This interview was taped on April 7, 1992, in Rudolfo Anaya's office at the University of New Mexico. R. S. Sharma teaches in the Department of English, Osmania University, Hyderabad, India.

RSS: Rudy, I am in this country to learn about the writers. You are one of the major voices of Chicano writing and, in fact, one of the pioneers. What exactly is meant by Chicano writing and Chicano literature?

RA: We are very glad that you can be with us. Welcome to the University of New Mexico in Alburquerque. [Anaya's recent novel is titled *Alburquerque.* He insists on using the original spelling of the city, la villa de Alburquerque.] The Chicano movement began in the mid-1960s in California and in the Southwest, and in other places where there were Mexican-American communities. It was designated as the Chicano movement because the Mexican-American community was looking for a word, a label, that would most closely fit our identity—our present identity. And so they took the word Chicano from *Mexicano;* Me-shi-cano became Chicano. Embodied in that word was a sense of pride, a sense of revolution, a sense that we had to create our own destiny, a sense that we could not leave that destiny in the hands of Anglo-America; we had a history and a heritage and a language to preserve, to be proud of and to study.

That history had not been presented to us in the educational system. For me, Chicano means taking our destiny into our own hands. We are Hispano in the sense that we are a Spanish-speaking group; we are Mestizos in the sense that we are Mexicanos who came up (either recently, or in the last generation, or many years ago) from Mexico. Our ancestors came through Mexico and became part of the Mexican mestizo (a blending of the European with the Native Americans). In my case, my ancestors settled here along the Río Grande and for many centuries learned from, lived with, and intermarried

142

with the Pueblo Indians. So Chicano also meant taking pride in the indigenous Native American roots that are a part of us.

RSS: Well, the question of tradition. Which tradition would you like yourself to be associated with? The European tradition, so-called American tradition, or the Spanish tradition in literature? Or would you like to create a tradition of your own?

RA: You said in your lecture last week that India is, in many ways, an eclectic country. That it draws from many traditions and maybe that's its strength. I see myself as an eclectic person. I can draw from many traditions. If we are really to know ourselves, we have to rely on the vast storehouse of humanity, not just one narrow path. As a matter of fact, that's been the problem in this country. In the United States, Anglo-America has insisted on the tradition of *one* path to follow. (The melting pot, you see.) It doesn't fit. It doesn't work and it creates damage and harm.

You also hit the nail on the head when you said, "Would you like to create a position of your own?" I think that is what the Chicano movement has done. We have looked at our heritage and our history and re-analyzed it to create a Chicano literature. So, for the first time through the publication of books that go out to society and to the world, we created a literature from our own community, from our roots. And in it we are speaking of our identity, our history, our language, the oppression that we have suffered, and we were pointing to the future. The sense of identity is what we would like to see in our community—to revitalize it, to give it pride, and to become, in a sense, this multicultural eclectic group that can draw from many streams of thought.

RSS: You have talked about bilingualism. And Chicanismo as a bilingual culture. Now, do you have problems with that? Do you think culture is language specific? If it is language specific which would you prefer, English or Spanish?

RA: One definition of culture is language specific: the language is the soul of the culture and if you lose the language, you lose the soul. I grew up speaking Spanish in a small village here in New Mexico. I spoke Spanish the first six years of my life, until I went to school. I didn't know a word of English. My grandparents and my parents spoke only Spanish, most of my family, most of the neighbors in that small village spoke Spanish. I still retain a great deal of my New Mexican Spanish and I speak it. Chicano youth of today are changing to English. I write now in English, as you know. I think what we can portray of our culture is now in the *content* of the story, the poem, or the play—in the content we can carry our culture and its values forward, even though the language is English. I would not like to see the Spanish language lost. I think we should preserve it, and I think this country should wake up and realize that being bilingual or multilingual is an asset and teach more language, but at the same time we're struggling with this very real contemporary problem: we have to do our best in English and see if the content will carry forth in that language.

RSS: Is the Chicano movement just a cultural movement? Are you just seeking cultural pluralism, or are you also seeking political pluralism? Do you have a politicalism now?

RA: Yes, we have a political agenda; it was especially evident in the early years of the Chicano movement. There were many ideologies that were presented to the Chicano community, ranging from Marxism to cultural nationalism, the myth of Aztlán, for example, and its power to perhaps regenerate and gather the community together again. Wrapped up in those ideologies were the ideals of more representation, better jobs, better health protection for farm workers, and other workers. We sought entry into post-secondary education, and we wanted an education that was relevant to our children in the lower grades. We desperately needed professors and administrators in secondary education and at the university level. All that was part of a very definite political agenda. Part of that political agenda was a parallel stream: the cultural movement. We returned to Mexican music, Mexican art and created Chicano literature, Chicano theater, motion pictures, and one of the most lasting attributes of the Chicano movement, Chicano literature. The Chicanos found their voice and began to publish in small presses, to create from the beginnings in 1965 a few books, and now twenty years later, hundreds of books and a whole new generation of writers, a whole new generation of women writers—Chicanas who are lending their perspective to Chicano literature.

RSS: Would you prefer a Chicano existence within the corporate life of the U.S. or would you like to be associated with life in Mexico?

RA: During the early days of the Chicano movement in the early 1970s I was traveling a lot to Mexico, almost every summer, and I was learning the culture and beginning also to speak more and more Spanish. I also studied the history and mythology, because I have made a great deal of use of mythology in my work. I like myth, the oral tradition that comes from the people and works its way into the novels. So, I was reflecting on the importance of that indigenous experience, whatever it is about me that is Mexicano. I filled myself up with those experiences, bringing them back with me to New Mexico where I was writing my novels.

My identity right now is tied to the Chicano identity. I can work in the Anglo-American world. I have been a professional teacher, secondary and also in the elementary, and the post-secondary schools at the university level. I can live in that world, I can work in it, I understand it. I could probably, after a very short time, also survive in Mexico, but my reality is here. My reality is in the United States as a person who has a particular history and heritage. Out of that heritage grew an identity that is strong, authentic, and proud. The United States should wake up and realize that those of us who are from different cultural groups want to keep up our identity within those groups, and we have every right to that identity.

You can see that I have a dark skin and features that don't fit the Anglo-American features, and you know that I was born here in New Mexico, my roots are here, so I demand to have a right to that identity. I can live in many cultures, and I can be multicultural and multilingual and still enjoy this identity. You see, the mainstream has tried to take that identity away from us. It didn't work. It caused too many problems and hardships and it ruined too many lives. People have to be free to choose their identity, so they can be fulfilled, so they can be liberated as authentic human beings.

RSS: The line of color, even in Mexico is not very well defined. In your writing you have recognized the Indian heritage as part of the Chicano heritage. Maybe as an American you have more in common with Anglo-America than with Mexico?

RA: I probably do. Because I was born and raised in this country. I am a product of its school system, I am a product of an English department at the university and majoring in English language and literature, and the psyche and the history and the popular culture and the racism of this country, so I am a product of this country. I don't deny that. And as you say, probably more so than of Mexico. I have lived here all my life. But I still have to create my own identity, and I want to preserve my Nuevomexicano culture and its values.

RSS: You are a writer. Who do you write for?

RA: Sometimes I write for the world, and sometimes I write for the Chicano community and sometimes that community is very specific. Sometimes I write for the Nuevo Mexicanos, the New Mexicans. Sometimes I will write either a scene or a passage thinking of a particular person enjoying that passage. Writing is a communication of my life to everyone. I am very much a part of this Southwest region. So I don't know if my work would strike a chord of recognition in India. But I hope it would, you see, because that's one of my goals, to write for everyone.

RSS: Yes. If literature did not have that universal element it will not register beyond its very immediate context. Many American ethnic writers are received very well in India, primarily because they have a great deal of feeling and emotion in their writing which is somehow missing in the mainstream. There is a great deal of experimentation with form.

RA: I would add to that that it's not only our emotion and our passion for writing, we are also presenting to the United States and to the world a particular world view.

RSS: What is that world view?

RA: For me, it's part European, it's part Anglo-American, it's part New Mexican, and it was formed in my childhood: the way of life that my parents and my grandparents lived, which was life in a small New Mexico village, a pastoral way of life with sheep, cattle, small farms along the river, very religious and spiritual. Religious and Catholic. Spiritual in the sense of oneness with the universe and the love of the earth which comes from the Native American traditions. A very communal approach to life, values of respect for the old, a very deep attachment to the earth that not only has to do with the pastoral lifestyle but, I think, it has to do with that Native American experience that the Mexicans learned in the Río Grande. The earth is the mother that nurtures us all with the grains and fruit which we receive. Add the fact that historically we were colonized in the mid-nineteenth century by the United States and you have added a brand new dimension to the world view of the Mexicano. And when two distinct world views and cultures meet, you get an added dimension to life not always pleasant. Sometimes borrowing and sometimes sharing and sometimes growing with each other, but also very often an oppressive situation which I think some Chicanos would insist is the true definition of Chicano. That dialectic between the Chicano and the Anglo-American.

RSS: Your work also grows from a strong house of myths and you're also creating myths. What are they?

RA: They are a way to understand the truth or to get to the truth. We want to understand the myths that all people have created on Earth, the spiritual myths of all communal groups. And maybe eventually we will learn the central storehouse of mythology. They're another way of looking at philosophy, spiritual thought, and wisdom. In my case they have to do with an indigenous experience. You know my book *Lord of the Dawn,* about Quetzalcóatl? It's based on a Mexican legend. I also have an interest in the cuentos (the oral tradition) of my culture. Native American myths resonate in me. They tell me something about myself. So I like to work those ideas into my novels.

RSS: Since the publication of your first novel you have done many other novels. Has your perspective as a Chicano writer changed?

RA: I would hope so. I am still very tied to the original idea I had of writing a literature that relates to my community, a literature that describes our experience—in which people can recognize themselves. My perspective has not changed. I have been labeled a regional writer. That used to bother me—it doesn't bother me anymore. Because I see the importance of the work that I'm, that we're, doing.

RSS: The label "regional writer" was perceived, and is still perceived, as limiting. But you have the literature of the East, the whole range of writers; you have the literature of the South.

RA: There is a whole world view wrapped up in the South that is defined by their history and their language and how they evolved. And we know so little about it. So we go to the writers and try to understand it. Through the literature we get a sense of their history. Someone said very recently, no one ever called Eugene O'Neill an ethnic writer. Of course he was, but he got incorporated into the canon, so it's much easier to marginalize us or pigeon-hole us and put us to the side and say "Oh, those are the ethnic writers," as if we didn't know anything. That's the problem of not accepting a more eclectic, multicultural point of view. Because then you don't give credit to each community and what it produces. To me that is hypocritical. As Chicanos we are here, and we are going to remain here and we're going to remain an active, creative people. The country will have to listen to us. We're going to make a difference.

RSS: Yes, I think there is a greater response to diversity in this country at the moment.

RA: There is also a reaction. While we have more people aware of diversity, and more classes in the universities, there is this big reaction against it. So we have to deal with both sides. The new openness and the old status quo.

RSS: In India we have fourteen constitutionally recognized languages with their own literature. So we are familiar with the phenomenon of diversity, literary diversity, which you are not. Our students, when they read Chicano writers, or American Indian writers, still think of them as American writers. Are you happy with that kind of perception?

RA: Yes, that's the way they see us in the beginning. But I think they have to dig deeper and realize the struggle that we've had within the society. We had to create our own literature and to create our own small presses. It hasn't been easy, you see. So, it's all right for your students to accept us that way, but also they have to know our history.

RSS: It would not appear to be true in your case considering that your first novel itself sold, if I'm right, more than a million.

RA: No, no, not a million. I think we're at 300,000.

RSS: That's quite a reasonable sale for a first novel.

RA: It's astounding in terms of book sales in this country. *Bless Me, Ultima* was published in 1972, it's now 1992, twenty years later . . . it's being used in high school, universities, around the world. I think many people still talk about it as a small press phenomenon. I'm very pleased. Now the publication houses of the United States are opening up a little bit to Chicano works. I see now that some of our writers are publishing with Doubleday, or Norton, or New Directions.

RSS: You mean there is a general acceptance of minority writing now in this country?

RA: In a limited way. Afro-American writing has had an acceptance for quite a while, published by the big trade publishers. A few Native American writers have had that acceptance, and are recognized. Chicano writers are still on the tail end. I would say it's only been in the past few years that major trade publishers will look at a Chicano writer or publish them. So, the general acceptance is still not there.

RSS: Who do you think are the major Chicano writers now?

RA: Maybe I'll give you a bibliography. That way you can look through the names. I think it's dangerous to talk about the *major* writers when we ourselves are struggling to get all the writers of our culture out and published. There has to be a real concern to make sure that women within our culture have access to publication, and that homosexuals and gays have access to publication. That people who have not been able to share in that process have

access. I think there is a new generation of young writers some of whom are
gaining in importance. We are going to have Denise Chávez here on Friday,
Ray González, Luis Urrea. José Montoya is still writing in California, one of
the members of the old generation, but still very active. I can go on and on.
There is now more of a gathering of other Latino writers in the United States.
I think you're going to see the Puerto Ricans and the Cubans really come
into the forefront and begin to learn about us and about each other. Virgil
Suárez, down in the South is doing an anthology and he published my work,
and he wants to come to New Mexico to make a connection with us. He's a
Cuban-American writer. The new Latino literature is going to be very excit-
ing in the next five or ten years.

RSS: But you will be still writing about the American experience. From a
different perspective.

RA: No, we will be writing—I will be writing about my experience *within*
the American experience. There's a difference.

RSS: I have read about Chicano writers. Chicano poets. Women writing
about literature, and I felt that many of them are writing the same way in
which other women were writing than, say, different ethnic groups. Anything
universal about this women's writing?

RA: I think if you talk to the Chicana writers their universal response has
to do with their struggle in a world that has been defined by men, and as
literature has been defined by men, and largely taught and propagated by
men. They have that common element. They are not presenting their own
voice, which is a new voice, very much like the Chicano male writers pre
sented their voice in the '60s and early '70s.

RSS: The ethnic writer wants to be heard. But you want something more
than simply being heard by an all-American audience.

RA: Well, isn't that idea of communication crucial to writing? In the beginning was the word, God wanted to be heard. Nothing wrong with a writer
wanting to be heard. Because being heard means being able to create in the
face of chaos (or in the case of oppression) your own identity. What is heard
in your voice and your voice says, I too am a human being! I, too, belong to
the human race and I have hopes and fears and aspirations: listen to me! I
think that is a very important element of why we dare to write.

RSS: I think there is too much reliance on the past in much of the ethnic
writing. Too much reliance on past history. Do you think there is a possibility
of looking beyond the past into the future?

RA: Writers writing about the future write science fiction, but I don't know too many ethnic writers writing science fiction. There's nothing wrong if your past has never been told, to tell it. We're trying to express our history, our community, our language, our language of the street, our bilingual language, everything that is us because it's never been told. This is what's exciting! We are concerned with the present and the future. That's where our children are going to live, and we have to give them skills to live in that world. But very many of us, or maybe I'll speak for myself, look at life now and into the future and don't see things I value. Life is getting more violent, more war, more greed, and we are creating technologies that enslave us instead of help us. So why shouldn't I look at values that came from my past, that speak to the human being and my needs, not only as a person but as a spiritual person? Nothing wrong with that. We read world literature and the classics and philosophy, not only contemporary literature, because history gives us clues to the search we have for our identity.

RSS: I didn't mean there was anything wrong in that pursuit. How do you relate to the present?

RA: My novel, *Alburquerque,* looks at my city, Alburquerque, New Mexico, at the traditional cultures of the Río Grande, at the Chicano, Native American, and what's happening all around us in the city. Change, new people coming here, new industry, money, politics, what all these have to do with my life and my community. The majority of the work that I see coming out now looks at and analyzes our present situation.

RSS: There's too much reliance, also, on myths and folklore. What do you think about form? Myth and folklore are very important ingredients of your form, of Chicano literature. Are there any new experimentations in form?

RA: Oh yes. Tremendous amounts of experimentation at the very beginning of the Chicano movement. Poets and writers were writing bilingual poetry, trilingual poetry, or poetry in four or five languages, English, Spanish, Black rhythm, Mexican Nahuatl, Indian, and our street Pachuco talk. [Nahuatl is the native language spoken in Central Mexico and Pachuco is the argot of the Mexican American (Chicano) zoot-suiters of the 1940s. Both languages are still spoken today.] Don't tell me that's not experimentation! It's been there from the beginning! In my own early novel, although it's a traditional story set in a small town in New Mexico, the Spanish language comes across as a crucial ingredient. Some of the newer writers now are very interested in experimenting with style. (Juan Felipe Herrera and Francisco

Alarcón are examples.) My own interest is still a more conventional approach to the novel because I want to communicate with my community. That's important to me, so I don't see my role as a stylist. My work comes from the oral tradition, mythology, magical realism, the community, all adapted to fiction.

RSS: I gather that the literacy percent is very low among the Chicano community. Do you think lots of people read the literature?

RA: I think many read, but unfortunately the history of the Mexican American people in this country tells us we have not had access to education. We have been a working people.

We have worked in farms and factories. Quite frankly, the generation after World War II and then my generation after the Korean War is the first Chicano generation to have widespread access to education. A small group of us became educated. Now we have a slightly larger group, the present generation, but it's still very low in comparison to the total society. So yes, literacy is a major concern in getting our stories, our poetry, and our theater out to our community. It is a major concern for me.

RSS: Do you have a kind of central body of Chicano writers? Something like the national association of Chicano writers?

RA: No. We have a National Association of Chicano Studies that meets once a year. Writers are asked to read and present panels on their work and we meet each other. We really don't have a national association of Chicano writers. It's a good idea.

RSS: What are the major journals devoted to Chicano writing?

RA: *Las Américas* from Arte Público Press and *The Bilingual Review* from the Hispanic Research Center in Tempe, Arizona State University, *La Confluencia* from Colorado.

RSS: Do you think a Chicano writer can live well by writing?

RA: No. As a matter of fact very few writers can live well, even to say, pay their rent and have food on the table, by writing. Most writers in this country do another job.

RSS: Do you feel satisfied as a writer? With your role as a writer?

RA: Extremely satisfied. I think it's the best life that the fates (el destino) could have granted.

RSS: I see that you have a large array of honors. What is your ultimate ambition?

RA: I don't have an ultimate. I have now a project to write four novels based on the city of Alburquerque. I have written about the idea of change, people trying to change New Mexico into their own image and the harm that comes to people already here. I've finished the second one, *Zia Summer,* about storehousing of nuclear waste in New Mexico. I'm working on the third one. So I would say short-term it's to finish this quartet of novels.

RSS: Are there writers writing plays, drama? Do you have a tradition of Chicano drama?

RA: Yes. We have a long tradition. In the old Mexicano newspapers of the Southwest, literature was included. And theater troops from Mexico used to come up and perform theater. We have folk theater and dances in the pueblos. And now we have the Chicano movement, teatro. Luis Valdez was very important in Chicano theater, and he's gone on to make movies. Jorge Huerta is very well known. We have here in Alburquerque a bilingual theater company that has produced some of my plays, and the plays of other writers, not only from the state but international writers. A good theater movement, struggling but good.

RSS: Thank you very much. I avoided asking you more universal questions, criticisms and theory because I wanted you to talk basically to reach out to the students and teachers.

RA: Well, it's also best, because, as you know, I think of myself as a writer.

Songlines of the Southwest: An Interview with Rudolfo A. Anaya

Ray González / 1993

From *The Bloomsbury Review,* Sept/Oct 1993: 3, 18. Reprinted by permission of publisher and Ray González.

This interview was conducted in March 1993 during Anaya's visit to The Guadalupe Cultural Arts Center in San Antonio, Texas.

The Bloomsbury Review: You're retiring from teaching at the University of New Mexico and want to devote more time to your writing and other interests. At the same time your novel *Alburquerque* is reaching a larger audience. It's going to appear in a mass paperback edition along with *Bless Me, Ultima.* Do you feel all these things show that you are reaching a new phase in your long career as a writer?

Rudolfo A. Anaya: That's a very good way to put it: a new phase. I don't view leaving the University of New Mexico and teaching as retirement. I view it more as the mid-career change, to do a lot of writing and other things, like reading. I want to do more essays. So I think it's just a shift of energy into new areas.

TBR: You are one of the first Chicanos to get recognition with *Bless Me, Ultima* in the early seventies, before the whole idea of multiculturalism meant a larger audience and more opportunities for Latino writers. Who do you think your audience was twenty to twenty-five years ago? Has it changed much? Are there more publishing venues than twenty years ago?

RAA: *Bless Me, Ultima,* was published in 1972, the same time that the multicultural efforts in education and publishing began. At that time *Bless Me, Ultima* had two audiences: one, the Chicano community, because they had not had contemporary fiction to read by living Chicano writers; two, white America found an interest not only in the culture I was portraying but also the worldview that was portrayed in my work. The audiences are still the same. There is a growing audience in the Chicano community that wants to read its writers, and certainly in twenty years we've built up that audience. It's more aware, and it's searching for new writers. The rest of the country has developed a tremendous interest in the cultural differences we present in our work. I also think an international audience has grown—there's an interest in Europe, in Mexico. I've gotten translations in Poland and Russia, for example. The cultural nucleus of family that we represent as Chicanos in the U.S. has so many fascinating and interesting aspects to it, that appeals to an international audience. That to me is a growing component.

TBR: When you were doing your early writing in the sixties and seventies, did you feel alone as a writer? Was there an external community back then or do you feel that now, with the higher attention on Chicano writers, there is more of a community?

RAA: Definitely, I felt very much alone as a writer. I was writing in Albuquerque, New Mexico, and teaching part time in grade school, then high school. I thought at the time, and I still do, that Chicano writers twenty years ago were composing the first models and aesthetics of what would be Chicano literature, for better or worse. I'll leave that to historical judgement. So we had that kind of isolation. We didn't have other contemporary works around us. It was the beginning of the whole Chicano movement.

In my case, I didn't have enough examples, especially in the novel. We had *Pocho* by Villareal, but even that we hadn't read. We really had to compose a style of our own, a sense of community, our sense of storytelling and the *cuentos, corridos,* the give and take of *familia.* We had to evolve that model that we would eventually present as our literature. The aspect that was not lonely was more of a subconscious energy; the Chicano movement itself. Literary movements are formed by this subconscious energy that is going on. You may not be aware of it, but you are being energized by it. By the time I hit the press in 1972 with *Bless Me, Ultima,* Quinto Sol was publishing Rolando Hinojosa and Tomás Rivera. Estela Portillo was also publishing. Out of that we created the base of contemporary Chicano literature.

TBR: Do you think that today *Bless Me, Ultima* offers its audience a chance to interpret the book differently than perhaps readers did twenty years ago?

RAA: I think that question could be better answered by critics from my point of view. They are still looking at the same things. In other words, teachers will tell me what their students think, or I'll get a group of letters from students, or I'll go to a high school and visit students. They are very interested in the life of Antonio, how he grew up, how it relates to them. They are interested in that element of our culture that is spiritual, that has to do with healing resources and with our long tradition of using the earth and its resources not only to feed ourselves but to heal us. All of that has come into a kind of fruition, and people are very interested. They still find the same kind of interest in *Bless Me, Ultima,* after all these years.

TBR: Even though there are more novels today by Chicano writers, the subject matter of *Bless Me, Ultima* is not found in too many of them. More of these contemporary novels are about urban life. The spiritual quest you offer in *Bless Me, Ultima* is harder to find in younger Chicano writers. Do you have any ideas of why that might be?

RAA: I think the movement from the rural to the urban setting is very natural. Chicanos have moved out of the farms, ranches, and small villages into urban settings. On the other hand, I insist that if there are universal values, that make us the community that we are, we have to take those universal values into the urban setting. Otherwise urban novels will reflect only chaos, violence, and disorientation of the contemporary urban setting. It's good too that writers reflect part of the realities as they try to give it meaning—as in *Alburquerque*—by not forgetting those roots. The roots of our universality as so deep and embedded in such a beautiful, indigenous tradition. Their fingers stretch back into Iberian and North African and Mediterranean traditions. We haven't begun to tap the deeper meaning of what constitutes our consciousness. That's what I find exciting—contemporary writers who will pay attention to what we can eventually call our *alma,* our soul, and reflect that in their work. There is so much to be done that we need dozens of writers poised to create the second phase of the Chicano movement, *una nueva onda.* We see it happening in the younger writers today. If we are going to reflect only on the disorientation and the chaos, then the question is, What do we reflect to our community? Part of my role as a writer is to reflect the deeper meaning of our universal experiences.

TBR: We've talked off and on about how there are more opportunities for younger Chicano writers. Do you ever wonder whether having more publishers going after their work, more agents, more reading and writing programs, take away from the sense of community among the writers? Can they get back to their people, or is there such competitiveness within the market that it removes the writers from their community?

RAA: I think it's natural in the evolution of any community to be caught up in the desires of the society at large. In many respects, its about time our writers had opportunities to publish with trade publishers that can distribute works to a wider audience. We write to communicate, and that communication somehow has to be gotten out. My only concern is that some of the publishers still view the Chicano community as one that really doesn't have depth of meaning, one still largely invisible to the American eye, invisible to white America. Exploitation may come about because they are now under pressure to publish the work of this community, which is big and growing. With the given world economics of this hemisphere, it is acquiring a force. We have to be careful not to join hands in that exploitation. We need our writers to be published and distributed. We need to make more movies, we need to get our music and art out because of our rich heritage. We have to remember one of our first jobs as Chicano artists is to try to reflect our own community and our own deeper reality of who we are as Chicanos.

TBR: You've written a number of other novels and several books of non-fiction, yet, *Bless Me, Ultima,* and its legacy are always with you and with readers and scholars of Chicano literature who know the history of the genre. How do you see yourself moving beyond that book and legacy, even though it's going to be a part of your biography forever? Has it been hard to live with that book and yet go on to other work?

RAA: Quite the contrary. Every author should be so lucky to have a first novel stay around twenty years. I see it as a blessing that I was able to write it in those early years while I was wrapped up in trying to find my soul within and the soul of my community, that I could pull enough together in one story to reflect that. People have told me that I'm lucky to hit that once in a lifetime. I was convinced as a young writer that what I wanted to do was go on and write, to try all kinds of genres, attitudes and attempts at storytelling. I've done nonfiction, travel journals, plays, and children stories. I learn more about myself and about writing by the constant exploration in those other areas. I'm darned glad I have a *Bless Me, Ultima* at the middle passage in my life. I can pay attention to a lot of things I want to write about. That's a very comfortable place to be.

TBR: When you read novels by other Chicano writers, especially younger ones, do you feel there is a sense of personal search or do you feel they are too busy reflecting on what's going on now, trying to be a part of the market and getting recognition? How do you approach these newer Chicano novels?

RAA: As I said earlier, I think it's part of a natural evolution to have this new bursting out, this flowering, this *nueva onda,* if you want to call it that, of young writers, especially a lot of women writers who are finding their voices. The only way we learn about ourselves is from a diversity of voices. You can't learn from one person. Even in the origin of our culture, we pay attention more to village elders as opposed to one chief priest. So we have that tradition, and new writers are the new chorus of the community. Being here, I was reflecting on how different San Antonio is from Albuquerque. We have to recognize that within the community we have these regional differences. We pay attention to different parts of our lives that have to do with the region and the landscape. We need the poets from San Francisco to read in New Mexico, and we need the writers from San Antonio to also read in New Mexico. They need us. That chorus is going to present a truer picture of who we are. In terms of the market, it is unwise for young writers to be fooled into exploitation by a market simply because it is there. Writing is an art. To me it's almost a sacred calling that we have. We are in the sense those new elders. We have to be careful that what we say is not exploited.

TBR: Albuquerque and the Southwest have been settings for a number of your books. In recent years, so-called border literature has been getting more recognition. Writers like Arturo Islas, Aristeo Brito, Denise Chávez, and yourself have been writing about this area. Why do you think there has been such a focus on the Southwest by novelists?

RAA: The ones you named live there. It is our turf, our *tierra.* One thing that makes writers strong is when they look at that field of energy, that *tierra* that has nurtured their body and their soul. It makes sense to write what you know.

TBR: Your most recent novel, *Alburquerque,* tells a different kind of history, of a familiar place to many people who either know New Mexico or have been to the area who like the Southwest. In many ways, it ties into your other novels like *Tortuga* and *Heart of Aztlan* because it continues to create and document a way of life that even many Chicano audiences may not be aware of. I sense *Alburquerque* is a very important novel in your career. It's gathered many things from your earlier work and put them into this story. How do you see the new book?

RAA: It is important in my career. You are right in saying it gathers the strands out of my first three novels. It is also quite a change in style for me. The lyricism I had as a young writer is not as prevalent. I saw myself moving into a new style by which to communicate to my community. Attacking political themes was something I hadn't done before. They certainly fit into the power struggles going on in the urban settings of the Southwest. The themes include problems of urban development that as an indigenous culture we have to deal with, and the growth of high technology in laboratories. The whole question will be with us forever—water usage, who owns, who dominates water usage, and how. In the West, it is a very important part of our lives. I'm in a new time and space. At the same time, I see that it has its roots planted in what is still *nuevo Mexicano*. The book is about what it means to me to be *nuevo Mexicano*.

TBR: Was it difficult to combine autobiographical details and the history of the area with these current political and environmental problems? How did you come up with a story that preserves that past as you take on current issues about growth in New Mexico?

RAA: It was difficult in the sense that I worked on the novel for ten years. That may be indicative of the process I was going through. I was doing a lot of other things: anthologies, writing plays, editing, doing a few children's stories. But I constantly worked on *Alburquerque* during those years. The changes in subject matter and style were not easy. They were earned.

TBR: You have also edited a number of anthologies and continue to publish *The Blue Mesa Review.* What made you go beyond the normal life of a writer to become an editor and work with different writers?

RAA: I have been fortunate since I first published in 1972. I owe some of my time and energy to the writing community. Anthologies are a way of bringing new voices out and publishing them. The anthologies I did were for small presses, and there was no money to be earned. I did them so the presses would be able to publish another book. It's giving back part of my good fortune to the writing community.

TBR: When I talk to other Chicano writers about what's going on in publishing now, with a growing audience, your name comes up when we ask who are the writers who need to be read, who are the writers you need to talk to and find out what it takes to survive. People who talk to you and read your books learn some of the things that you've gone through. You are now one of the elders you mentioned earlier, one of the first ones who broke ground for those of us today. Are you still learning things yourself, or are you just passing things on to other writers?

RAA: Every day I sit down in front of my computer to write something new or revise something. I'm learning. If I weren't learning every day, I wouldn't be writing. The process for me is one of self-illumination. My goal is clarity. That's the basis of my worldview and was taught to me by my ancestors. It's my way of being in touch with the community, the earth, the universe. That process is good whether you are an eighteen-year-old writing your first short story or fifty-five and working on a new novel. People call me up and send me manuscripts. I try to help as much as I can because it's again part of that return. They may be at a level where they need a lot of help. I'm willing to give as much as I can. Chicano writers by and large are still not coming out of the MFA creative writing programs. We're still largely self taught. We need to help each other a lot. The most important thing you can give a young writer is an editorial vision about what the work has in it, how it can be improved, what you see happening. If I were going to set up a program to help young Chicano writers, I would set up a mentorship program between young and older writers so that they could work together for six months to a year. The give and take is helpful.

TBR: In the beginning of the interview we talked about your being in an important place in your career—reading, getting away from teaching, finding more time for the other things. Are there any projects or goals you have not reached yet?

RAA: I have in mind a quartet of novels: *Alburquerque* is the first one, *Zia Summer* is the second one. I've already written it. I'm starting now to work on the third one. The goal of a quartet is brand new, and it's going to take a long time. I want to shift a bit of attention into developing stories for children, because one of the most crucial areas where we can give our sense of community is to the *niños,* to the young people. It's a responsibility that we have. I also want to continue to travel and do readings. Maybe spend more time in my apple orchard.

TBR: You've been in New Mexico your entire life, and you've produced a body of work mainly set in New Mexico. You've taught there and continue to create there. You are a writer who has a real sense of place. That's hard to find in a lot of writers today. Is there anything about home that means the most to you as you look back on your career?

RAA: If you study the map, you will find there are certain migration routes that are used along what we call the *frontera.* Our ancestors used these routes because they were what the aborigines of Australia called the "songlines of the earth," the songlines of *la Madre Tierra's* memory. The Río Grande valley and the Sangre de Cristo mountains in New Mexico for me are those kinds of places on earth. There is a great deal of spirituality attached to places. The sense of the memory of my ancestors and the memory of the earth is what gives me my power to write and reflect upon it. So I can't see uprooting myself in search of something new when it's right at my back door. Or I would say my door that faces east where the sun comes up every morning over the Sandia Mountains.

Anaya Explores Sexuality, Mid-life Crisis in New Play

Rubén Sosa Villegas / 1994

From the World Wide Web, 23 January 1994. Reprinted by permission of Rubén Sosa Villegas.

DENVER - Exploring themes of mid-life crises and sexuality among middle-aged Chicanos inspired noted author Rudolfo Anaya (*Bless Me, Ultima* and *Alburquerque*) to write the play *Ay, Compadres.*

"In the Chicano community very little has been done for the middle-age group," said Anaya, who will premiere *Ay, Compadres* at Denver's El Centro Su Teatro this spring.

"It involves two couples that are compadres (godparents) and basically it's an evening at home," Anaya said. "One couple has invited the other couple. And they've been compadres for 21 years.

"They've done a lot of things together and traveled together. And they get along very well, but they're at a point of going through their midlife crisis. The women have gone through menopause and the men are going through male menopause."

Anaya approached the subject with caution.

"It takes a candid look at this subject which very often isn't discussed in the community or in our relationships," Anaya said. "We don't often talk about our midlife crisis. We tell lies, shrug it off or build these fences."

To tear down those fences, Anaya used mirth.

"It's a comedy," Anaya said. "It's a way of looking at the subject matter and bringing it out in public but at the same time treating it in a light-hearted way."

Anaya wrote the story as a play after visualizing a scene in which two couples are sitting together one evening playing cards and grilling hamburgers.

"I had an idea of them discussing more social and cultural issues," Anaya said. "But then the idea of treating the sexuality theme became very important to me, especially from the point of view of people in middle age. We

161

certainly have writers that treat sexuality in their twenties and thirties, and it was the big problem with AIDS, I think, that caused the world of sexuality to be very public now. People are talking about it."

Ay, Compadres is a two-act play that "was a lot of fun to write," Anaya said. "Some works just say 'I'm a short story' and some say 'I'm a play' and some say 'I'm a novel,' and this one just said 'We want to be on stage. We want to have these middle-age compadres and comadres on stage this evening and then getting into the whole idea of what sexuality means in their life in the mid-50s." So there's a few movidas chuecas (crooked moves) going on there and it's part of the fun, I hope.

"The Chicano community has always been one that really inspires me to write, so it's always been fun to be there when they see it for the first time and to get their reaction," Anaya said. "People say that I'm pretty cool on the exterior, but anybody who writes and then you have the public judge your work, you get nervous inside. And I suppose the more difficult the subject is, the more nervous one is apt to get.

"There may be other plays like this, treating the subject matter, but I haven't seen them. If there are, there are very few. So it's a new space to get into and create in. You don't know if all the compadres and comadres out there are going to cheer you on or throw tomatoes at you."

So far, Anaya has avoided the tomatoes. Five years ago, his play *Who Killed Don Jose?,* a murder mystery, was staged. Last year it was *Matachines,* a play that included the old Spanish ritual dance of the same name. And last month director Ramón Flores staged Anaya's *The Farolitos of Christmas* in Albuquerque.

Anaya's newest play, *Billy The Kid,* may be staged this year.

"There's a lot of interest in *Albuquerque,*" Anaya said. "It has been read, and there's a producer and a few actors who would really like to get it (*Billy The Kid*) off the ground.

"It's a completely different play because it treats the subject matter—that everyone recognizes Billy The Kid—but we've done it from a Nuevo Mexicano (New Mexican) point of view. We know that Billy The Kid spoke Spanish. He got along well with the Mexicanos in Lincoln County, and I would hear stories when I was a kid about him going to Puerto de Luna where my parents were born and raised.

"And all the stories I always heard were favorable. They called him 'El Billito.' I said: 'Why not take a look at that from a new point of view instead of what we usually see.' I'm pretty excited about that one, too. But, of course, that's not in the production stage yet."

Anaya's most popular novel, *Bless Me, Ultima,* also has been staged twice. Its most recent appearance was last year at the Plaza de la Raza cultural activities center in Los Angeles.

"They did a fantastic job," Anaya said of the adaptation. "It was great, especially when you consider that these were barrio kids."

Anaya is currently writing two novels, both murder mysteries. "They have a New Mexico setting and very definite cultural context in terms of social, political, and personal interactions of what's going on in the Southwest."

Warner Books will release *Bless Me, Ultima* in hardcover this spring and will release *Alburquerque* in paperback this fall. The hardcover dust jacket for *Bless Me, Ultima* is illustrated by Santa Fe artist Bernadette Vigil.

"My work is going to get a little wider circulation this year," Anaya said. "My work will get more distribution and be more accessible to people, which is what it's all about. I'm looking forward to it."

A Conversation with Rudolfo Anaya

Laura Chavkin / 1995

From *Indiana Review,* Spring 1997, 41–53. Reprinted by permission of publisher and Laura Chavkin.

This interview took place in Albuquerque, New Mexico, on 10 August 1995.

LC: Can you tell me a little about your background and your career?

RA: I was born in New Mexico. Actually, I was born in a very small town, Pastura, which, by the way, worked its way into my first novel *Bless Me, Ultima.* I was raised in Santa Rosa, which is on the eastern side of the state. I went to school there through the eighth grade. It's a small town on Highway 66. I spent most of my childhood either going to school or playing along the river, or in the hills playing with friends, or listening to community and family telling stories. I guess that's when I got my yearning to be a writer, although I didn't know it at the time.

My family moved to Albuquerque in 1952, after World War II. That was happening to a lot of the communities in the state. People were going to bigger cities where there was more opportunity for work, and so we left the small town and wound up in Albuquerque. We lived in a barrio which is called Barelas.

LC: Can you tell me what motivates you to write?

RA: I've always said that all people have a creative spirit. We're all creative in one way or another. I guess in my case reading a lot and finding ideas in literature and being a student at the university as a young man and trying to emulate some of the poetry and stories that I was reading sparked that spirit of creativity. At that point in my life I was introverted, quite alone, and so writing was a way of expressing my feelings, my ideas. Reading the ideas of others slowly worked its way into looking back on my childhood and seeing it as something that I could use as the subject matter for a novel.

LC: When did you decide you wanted to become a writer?

RA: I don't think that's a decision that was very clear cut in my life. I really trained to become a teacher because that meant that I could get a job.

I knew very little about the life of a writer, where you went to work, or what would happen if you just sat around and just wrote stories. In a sense I was pragmatic about my education and getting a degree that I could use. I was writing all the time at night, and so it was an evolution instead of an overnight decision. My writing evolved.

LC: When you first started writing, were there any writers who influenced your work or served as models?

RA: Almost everyone that I read, especially during my university years, I would say was important because that's when I really realized the power of literature. I was reading everything, everyone.

LC: Do you write for yourself, or your family, or friends, or an ideal reader?

RA: Writers write to communicate their ideas, so their audience is always the widest audience possible. I think there are times when we might focus in on a family, group, or community, but at the same time the story or whatever we're working on has to make a leap to the world.

LC: Are you conscious of a political message when you write? Do you deliberately try to include a social message or political message in your fiction?

RA: Probably so, since we live in a social and political context, we can't help but respond to it, and perhaps all that is wrapped up in our literature. I think the difference is how one does it. If it's a goal of a writer to be very direct about conveying a social and political message, that's one way to approach literature. On the other hand, one's atmosphere, one's social life, feelings, or ideas about the society can also appear in more subtle ways in what one writes.

LC: Are any of your stories somewhat autobiographical?

RA: I think my first three novels are the most autobiographical because there I am in settings that I know intimately, and I'm using people I knew as models for characters. After the first three novels, it seems that I begin to get away from a very strict autobiographical setting. On the other hand, characters always reflect the author so writing never quite escapes autobiography.

LC: Is there a religious foundation for your works?

RA: I think there is a spiritual foundation in my work.

LC: What do you see as your particular strength as writer? Do you see any weaknesses you'd like to correct?

RA: Oh, sure. Writing is, for me at least, never completely learned, and so every manuscript I do, I revise over and over, and I'm always learning. It's a process of learning and every element that there is in fiction I can always improve on.

LC: How elaborate are your outlines before you begin writing? Do you depart much from your original plans?

RA: I don't do outlines.

LC: Where is your greatest effort made? In your first draft or in the subsequent revisions?

RA: The first draft. If I can put a lot of time and concentrated energy and focus into that first draft, once I have that draft I am relieved because revision is a lot of work, but it's a good feeling to have that first draft done.

LC: At what part do you begin revising? Do you write a whole draft and then rewrite or do you revise as you write?

RA: I finish a complete manuscript, and then I start revising. I have to add that now that we use computers it's easier to revise while working on a first draft. I find myself doing that. I'll be on chapter ten and I'll go back and straighten out chapter two. With the computer I can just flip over to it and revise it.

LC: When you compose a novel, do you find yourself moving scenes to different parts of the novel as you write the various drafts?

RA: I don't do that much in the first draft. The first draft usually seems to flow, and the scenes seem to come where they should be. But when I revise, there's always the possibility that I'll take out scenes or move them.

LC: Would someone comparing your early drafts with your published story gain insight into your process of revision or thinking?

RA: Oh, yes, anyone might learn a lot by comparing the first draft to the published version. Since I really try to get through the first draft to have it in hand, to finish it, the first draft is usually very rough. The process of revision shows how ideas and symbols come from the subconscious and then are refined in revisions. To me that's a very important process, so anyone looking at those different drafts can get an insight into the working of my mind.

LC: Do you get advice and suggestions for changes before you submit a story for publication?

RA: Yes. It's important who is giving the advice. The person that I trust to give me that advice happens to be my wife. I'll finish a manuscript, and I'll give it to her to read and she'll give me her feedback on it.

LC: Can you describe a typical working day?

RA: On a typical working day, I get up, take a walk, have breakfast, and ask my wife if there's any work I need to do like washing dishes before I start writing. I write for about three hours and then have lunch and then spend the afternoon either answering letters or doing community work or projects or going visiting schools.

LC: Do you try to write seven days a week?

RA: I used to write seven days a week and through the holidays. Recently, I give myself more breaks on weekends, and I'll take a weekend off and maybe go to the mountains and just get away from work.

LC: How many pages can you write on an average day?

RA: When I am working on the first draft of an original manuscript, it would be maybe three or four pages.

LC: Do you ever write in long hand or always use a word processor?

RA: Word processor.

LC: Do you complete a project before moving on to the next one or do you work on several things at the same time?

RA: I can work on a couple of projects at the same time but not novels. If I'm working on a novel, I can't be working on two novels. I could be working on a novel and a children's story or a novel and an essay. That works. I can do that.

LC: Some writers have stated that writing is a painful, exhausting, and frustrating process for them; what's your experience?

RA: It is painful; there is a lot of intense mental work involved, but it's also a meditative type of work. One learns to focus one's mental energy. It's also a process of discovery. We learn about ourselves, we learn about human nature, and I think in a sense that's why I write, that process is a journey of revelation.

LC: Which of the works gave you the most trouble to write and which was the easiest?

RA: I think the novel I spent the most time on was *Alburquerque.* One reason it took so long is because I was also doing a lot of other literary projects like editing magazines, helping put together anthologies. I wasn't concentrating on it entirely. None of them were easy; they all took a lot of time and love.

LC: How do you relax after a day of writing?

RA: I have a garden, and I go out and water the trees and grass. I read a lot in the evenings. I really like to read. On the weekends I like to get away to the mountains. I have a cabin up there where I can get into a different setting and meet different neighbors and relax. I also have a granddaughter who has a horse so we spend a lot of time with her and her schoolwork. Anything that's not writing is a break.

LC: Does it disturb you that your work prompts different reactions and interpretations?

RA: No, that's what literature should do; that's what all art should do. Exactly that—prompt people to respond to it, and certainly everyone has his or her own opinion.

LC: What aspects of your work have been neglected by the critics?

RA: I don't know. Critics will do what they want to do; that's kind of their business so I don't get too involved in that.

LC: Many critics today think a writer has an obligation to become involved in politics and social issues. What do you think about that point of view?

RA: Yes, I think that's very important. We live in a time that is extremely volatile. There is a lot of hate, prejudice, and bigotry that we see throughout the world. We see communities turning against each other, and so I think it's important for us to speak of those issues and perhaps lend our sense of what is right, how to understand each other better, and how to solve problems. Those things can be incorporated into our work.

LC: Do you think the government should subsidize writers with grants from the National Endowment for the Arts?

RA: Yes, I do. I think that a very active commitment by any level of government to its community, especially that community that is creating the arts of the community, is important. There's so much to say about that subject; it's an investment that I think has been made throughout history. It is critical that a society sees the importance of the arts and the humanities and invests in them. If we take that away, we're taking part of the knowledge that we gain about ourselves, given that perspective from the arts.

LC: Part of the research project I'm working on for the National Endowment for the Humanities is examining literature for values that Americans from different ethnic backgrounds share. Do you think there are any shared American values?

RA: Yes, there are. In the sense that history, literature, and any kind of communication media, and what we call popular culture, education, and language, all of those social forces create shared values. If one lives in this country, one is aware of them. They are all around. I think what is going on in this country now is that those shared values are being analyzed, and what the country needs to realize is that there are a lot of different communities and regions—including gender communities—that have a perspective to plug into those shared values that perhaps have never been heard before. If there's a revolution going on in this country, it's that sense of communities wanting to be heard, to be recognized, to be seen, and they are saying that "our view of the world, our value system is also important, and here's what we have to offer."

LC: How does one reconcile his or her ethnic background with American culture which sometimes seems to demand assimilation?

RA: That's the issue that this country must address, and it's an issue that has been around for a long time. Now we are dealing with it again. It comes back to what I said earlier. There are communities that present their world view, their perspective on life, and still understand the dominant culture system, the dominant culture's values. When I look at the history of the world and at places where different cultures and nationalities have met, and when one culture desires to impose itself on the other by demanding assimilation, there's bound to come an explosion from that type of repression. It seems to me that what is healthier for a country as it evolves its values is to not force those other communities within its border to all be the same. It's that force of assimilation that people eventually react against. It seems that a kind of shared value system, sharing back and forth, understanding back and forth, a kind of growth that is fluid and organic is much healthier in the long run than anything that tries to assimilate through repression.

LC: Did you think much of your Mexican American heritage when you were growing up or did you take it for granted?

RA: We pretty much took it for granted because here in New Mexico the Mexican American heritage has had a long history and it's been very strong and very obvious. I think the only time we were made to think about it was when we didn't fit in somewhere. If something happened at school, and we didn't fit in, then we would wonder, "Why am I different, what's wrong with me? Why can't I take a part in that play? Maybe I do have an accent, but why didn't I get the leading role?" In my case, when I started at the university there were very few Chicanos there, and I was the only one studying English Language and Literature. I remember some instances I felt really different. I remember when somebody told me "you speak with an accent," and so those were instances when I was made aware that I was Mexican American.

But within my family and community, it was just a pretty good feeling. That's just the way we grew up, that's how we communicated, that's how we understood the world, and it was great, a very rich kind of heritage and dynamic living culture to be in. It still is, but there are still those problems. We're often reminded that we're different, and a lot of times that doesn't come in a positive way. "To be different" comes attached with prejudice, negative feelings, and bigotry. That's what education, teachers, and artists in this country have to address. Why can't we be different and still be accepted?

LC: How would you define an American?

RA: An American? Probably anyone who lives from the Arctic Circle to Tierra del Fuego.

LC: When did you begin writing your first book, *Bless Me, Ultima?*

RA: I began writing it in the early sixties.

LC: William Faulkner had explained that the origin of *The Sound and the Fury* was a symbolic mental picture. Do you recall how *Bless Me, Ultima* began, what prompted it?

RA: I had written a lot of stories and novels that all seemed to be imitative of the kind of literature that I was reading at the university as an undergraduate student. In that process, I shifted my focus to childhood to write stories of a young boy, putting myself perhaps in the role of one of the characters. That process was long and involved and when one of the characters, Ultima, came to inspire my writing process, to inspire the novel, to inspire me, that's when the novel suddenly acquired a focus.

LC: Why do you think *Bless Me, Ultima* has prompted so much controversy?

RA: Does *Bless Me, Ultima* stir up so much controversy?

LC: Yes. Some people want it banned from public schools.

RA: I think that in the case of public schools, there are still some very narrow views of what literature is and what literature should be taught in this country. I also think that the people who have rejected it are a very small minority. We think that there are more of them because they make more noise, but most people that I know want a really good education for their children, and they are aware that the world is multicultural. This country is multicultural and the more their children know about other communities not only the better off will they be communicating with those communities, but they will have a better life in terms of future work.

Narrow-minded people read *Bless Me, Ultima* and instead of seeing how it might present a picture of another community they focus on the "strong language." They say, "we don't want our kids to read strong language." Or they say, "this man writes about witchcraft and we don't want our kids to read and write about witchcraft." Both of those objections miss the boat entirely.

It's not what the novel is all about. People have told me that the levels of language are all around us, and if kids are going to learn them, kids don't need *Bless Me, Ultima*. Language is just all around us. Another teacher told me and told a group of parents, "*Bless Me, Ultima* is not a manual on witchcraft." It happens to be the central theme of the book so it provokes controversy for people who look for those nit-picky areas to criticize.

On the other hand, the interesting controversy is the critical work that people write about *Bless Me, Ultima*. This form of critical thinking is very healthy because it's about the different themes and symbols in the novel and the meaning and decisions that Antonio has to go through. In fact, high school students send me letters from all over the country. They have read the novel, and they quickly get beyond the strong language and get to the themes in the novel. That kind of critical controversy and viewpoint is very good.

LC: Do you think that the pagan religion of the Golden Carp and Catholicism in *Bless Me, Ultima* conflict in life today?

RA: Yes, they do in the sense that the Catholic religion in *Bless Me, Ultima* is very dogmatic. It has a dogma that must be adhered to and followed. The Golden Carp that Antonio sees as the alternative doesn't have that dogma, and, of course, they're going to be in conflict.

LC: Did you ever have a conflict with the Catholic religion like Antonio?

RA: I can't say that it was exactly like Antonio's. I think that in a sense the novel is autobiographical. I identified very strongly with Antonio while I was writing the novel. I was asking myself again all those questions that are very pertinent to life. The novel has to do with the meaning of good and evil and the nature of God, our purpose in life and the whole idea of the sacred. What is the sacred and how can we respond to it in a spiritual way? So yes, those are questions that I have always asked myself and have had to resolve for myself. If that is conflict, then that is a conflict that promotes growth because it allowed me to find my own spiritual way.

LC: You are usually regarded as the father of Chicano literature. Do you feel any anxiety because of this?

RA: No, not one bit of anxiety. It's a title someone gave me as an honorary title, and I accept it graciously.

LC: Can you tell me about the flowering of Chicano literature in the 1960s?

RA: That was the era of the Chicano movement, and it was an era in which we created a contemporary literature and brought it out of the oral tradition where it had been and put it into print so that it could be more widely disseminated. It is one of the most important literary movements of this country, and I think that this country has not paid enough attention to that movement. I don't know why. The Hispanic population in this country is really big; when any community produces a flowering of literature like we did, it should be of great interest to everyone.

LC: Do you think it is useful to study Chicano writers as a group, as people do in the universities?

RA: Yes, I do, in the same sense that in different departments you can study French literature, Mexican literature, Russian literature, Afro-American literature, or literature by women. There is something about the history of the community that is important to learn, and a class called Chicano literature can give it that focus and bring into play the history of the people, their relationship to the mainstream culture, and a lot of other relevant material that makes literature more meaningful as you read it. All that takes time. That's why you need the focus of classes aimed at the study of Chicano literature.

LC: What common themes or concerns do you think unite Chicano writers?

RA: The language, the history, the folklore, the mythical beliefs underlying the multicultural roots that are our heritage, the relationship that we have to Anglo-America, the encounter with Anglo-America that occurred in the mid-nineteenth century, the continuing sense of tension between the two communities. The shaping of the world view and how it is different for the Chicano and different for the Anglo-American creates a constant but very interesting kind of tension.

LC: You mentioned the oral tradition before, can you comment on how that has influenced your work?

RA: The oral tradition is how our history was passed down to us. It's extremely important. It's like reading a book on the history of the United States and learning what your tradition is like. For us, a lot of that was wrapped up in the family and community stories that were told. We also learned a lot of techniques from the way the story is told. For me, it's been very important.

LC: Some people believe that it's more difficult to write a good short story than a novel. Do you believe that?

RA: Not really. I think you can define a short story as a precious little gem that if it all comes together it must have taken you an incredible amount of focus and energy. That's fine, and I'll agree with that definition, but each scene in a novel can take the same amount of concentration.

LC: The settings seem especially important in your work. Did any of your stories evolve by your settings?

RA: All of my stories seem to resonate with the setting. The stories usually evolve out of characters, but the characters seemed so tied to their landscape that I'm sure the reader will feel that the inspiration of the landscape came first.

LC: Did you like teaching creative writing courses? Do you think teaching interfered with your writing?

RA: No, I enjoyed very much teaching creative writing. I always had time left over at night to continue my own writing. It worked as a career for me.

LC: Do you feel that people can be taught how to be creative writers in courses?

RA: I feel that people come to classes or to groups to have someone respond to their work. If you put in a year or two or three into writing something, and you get no feedback, it can be a very lonely feeling. As people respond to your work, you get ideas of where you're going and perhaps how to improve on it. In that sense, it's valuable.

LC: What kind of advice would you give to beginning writers?

RA: I always tell writers to read a lot, to look at the way other writers construct stories, to look at techniques and feel passionate about how writing as an art and how much it can convey, can move you. If you have that passion and that's going to stir your own creativity, that's all you need because that's the bottom line, the desire that one has to communicate in an artistic way.

LC: What kind of influence did your education have on your writing? Were your English classes helpful?

RA: Yes, because I was reading a lot, and for the first time I was finding that there were all these wonderful ideas in literature. There were all these wonderful ways to speak about it, and all of that was very helpful.

LC: What approach would you take if you were teaching a course in fiction?

RA: Teaching a course in fiction or creative writing?

LC: Creative writing.

RA: In creative writing I always had my students outline a project they wanted to finish, and then we would start by developing the characters and the beginning of a story and kind of going from there, letting it evolve. What happens to that character, what kind of person is that character, and the more you learn about that person, the more that story grows.

LC: Do you find it difficult to write from the point of view of the opposite sex?

RA: I have done only one novella from the point of view of a woman, *The Legend of La Llorona,* and yes, it is difficult to get into that complete world and to reveal it. I think in some of my plays I try that.

LC: Do you find it useful to talk with other writers? Are your friends writers? Do you talk shop with them?

RA: I have a lot of friends who are writers, and I get involved with organizations that help writers. A lot of times I'll read manuscripts for beginning writers, but most of my friends are teachers or plumbers or cowboys.

LC: Some writers begin their novel by writing the opening and the end of the novel. When you write a novel, do you write from beginning to end or do you skip around?

RA: I write from beginning to end.

LC: Has success changed your attitude toward life or toward your work?

RA: It's taught me to be grateful that so many people have read my work and have either told me or written me that it has a great deal of meaning for them. That has made me perhaps more aware of a kind of responsibility to all people.

LC: I've read that you'll be publishing some children's books. Can you tell me how that interest came about?

RA: I have a granddaughter that spends a great deal of time with us, and every night when she's staying with us, I tell her a bedtime story. And suddenly I realized that some of those stories were worth writing so I put them in a computer and began to get very interested in the fact that there had been very few children's stories written for the children from our community. Children who are pre-school age or in the early grades do not see themselves in stories, and they should. I thought it was really important to develop writing in that area, so I've been writing in that area.

LC: You've been labeled an ethnic writer. Does that label disturb you?

RA: No. I think what is disturbing is why only certain communities are called ethnic writers. First of all, when we call ourselves Chicano writers, we feel very good about that. We feel proud because we are developing a literature for our community. The other side of that is that we do wonder sometimes why only some people are ethnic writers. Many have said they don't call Eugene O'Neill an ethnic writer. But they call Chicanos "ethnic" writers. It's a term I think one has to be very careful with. I've seen it used to demean writers. To some critics, when they put that label on writers, they imply that literature is not worth looking at. It can be a loaded term.

LC: Can you tell me about your work in progress?

RA: I just published a novel called *Zia Summer.* I don't know if you've seen it.

LC: Yes, I have.

RA: That's my first murder mystery, and I created this young man who's the private investigator. I'm doing a series on him. My work in progress has to do with Sonny Baca and the series of novels he's involved in. I've also finished a short novella which will come out in February, 1996, *Jalamanta, A Message from the Desert.* It's a philosophical novella, and I outline my sense of the sacred in that novella. I've been writing children's stories and just had a play produced, and if I had time I'd write another play. So I've had lots of things to do.

LC: Thank you for giving me the opportunity to talk with you today
RA: Thank you.

An Interview with Rudolfo Anaya

Bruce Dick and Silvio Sirias / 1997

Conducted by telecom from Boone, North Carolina, 1997. Copyright
Bruce Dick, Silvio Sirias, and Rudolfo Anaya.

Dick: Looking back on twenty-five years of giving interviews, how do you
feel about statements you made years ago that seem to live forever in print?

Anaya: I often think that people who do interviews don't realize that people change and go through different phases. Writers change as well. I was at
a different place when I wrote *Bless Me, Ultima.* I'm in a different place now.
I'm writing murder mystery books and children's books, and I think that it is
very important for the people who read past interviews to be aware of these
different phases of life. This is particularly true with regard to how one views
one's writing and what one has learned, or not learned, along the way.

Dick: In past interviews you have mentioned that you often incorporate
mythic elements into your fiction. Here is a quote that illustrates this point:
"There is a story line or plot on one level and then there are other levels that
seem to be speaking to me." How do your detective novels, the Sonny Baca
series, figure in to this mythology?

Anaya: If you read all three novels that answer will become very clear
because Sonny is involved with a group of people who are initiating him into
shamanism and he doesn't realize that at first. He knows that the *curanderas*
are part of his culture, and Don Eliseo has a kind of wisdom that aligns him
with the seasons, the earth, and his Pueblo Indian neighbors nearby. But he
hasn't really tapped the mythic origin of what is going on around him because
he has lost those roots in the process of becoming educated, of joining, to a
certain degree, the mainstream way of being. Once you read the three novels
you realize that what Sonny is doing is returning to those origins. If he is
able to return to his origins he can become as powerful as Don Eliseo. Those
origins have to do with the mythic element of life, with the journey that
illuminates what is beneath your feet all of the time and illustrates how one
is connected to all those universal stories, all that universal mythology that
flows in our blood.

Sirias: The Sonny Baca murder mysteries read as if the detective novel
was a genre that you found fun. Is that true?

Anaya: In writing *Zia Summer* I had a lot of fun. I discovered that the genre was interesting, that I could slap-stick all sorts of things into it, that I could incorporate cliff-hanger at the endings of chapters, that I could have Sonny dashing around, getting into trouble, into fist fights, getting nearly killed. I enjoyed that type of writing and the revision it involved. It was fun. And it was also fun because the voice of the novel seemed to be saying, "Wow, you are really communicating with your audience!" Writing the Sonny Baca series was like watching an enjoyable movie. You chuckle and you're engaged in its development. I felt this book was going to communicate with my audience. I didn't think so much of following the prescriptions of the detective genre. I was in part learning what a murder mystery is all about, but I was more interested in conveying a cultural context, a tradition, a history, and that was also fun. In fact, my wife says, "You really aren't writing murder mysteries, you're kind of using the elements of the genre to do what you have always done. There is not much difference between Sonny Baca and some of your other characters of the past. They have all been on this journey to find out what their potential really is in the end."

Dick: Do you agree with your wife's statement?
Anaya: Yes. I agree with everything she tells me. (Chuckle).

Dick: In the past you've mentioned that you never conduct research because to research is to borrow somebody else's words. Did you research the detective novel when you decided to write the Sonny Baca series?
Anaya: No, I didn't.

Dick: It came to you in an inspiration?
Anaya: I think we are exposed to all forms of writing, whether it be through television, the movies, or the written word. I always remember growing up and watching a lot of movies. If you're observant you internalize how to create a plot, build characters, develop a story line. You don't need much more than that. Then you hear stories that people tell, and you read. So I didn't see the genre as that different, or as one that I wanted to control me, to put limitations on me as a writer. I saw it more as a vehicle to communicate Sonny's story, which is the story of the Albuquerque community. This in turn has all sorts of cultural, linguistic, and educational implications in terms of the technique of the novel. I didn't need to acquire this by reading mystery novels.

Sirias: The relationship Sonny has with the police rings especially true. It's not central to the plot, but it looks like you had to do some homework to become familiar with that.

Anaya: One thing I did was to visit the police station here in town and talk to a couple of detectives. They were extremely nice. They took me around the lab, showed me their guns, and showed me what they do. At the time I thought that I should read a lot of mystery novels. But I think the instinct of the writer is always just to jump into the work, especially if it has a kick to it, if it has something to say. I rely on character, which I know is anathema for a postmodernist, but who cares. In our community the identity of the character is important. So when my character is authentic, sitting right next to me when I'm writing, involved in the scene, and is having as much fun as I am, then I don't need the ninth degree of research. What caliber of pistol did he use? If I get it wrong, I'll call someone.

Sirias: Speaking of character, would you consider Sonny Baca your most memorable character since Ultima?

Anaya: I think in a strange way he will become the most memorable since the Antonio-Ultima pair in *Bless Me, Ultima.* I say that because I am getting feedback from people who come to me and talk about him as if he's real. They ask me, "Did you know him?" Women tell me, "I would like to meet Sonny Baca, he sounds really exciting." That tells me that he is coming across as a very authentic character, that he's touching the consciousness and perhaps the passions of my readers.

Dick: How has the Sonny Baca series been received?

Anaya: I think the critical response is very different from the popular response, and I guess I am more interested in the popular response. I am more interested in what the people I write for tell me about the characters.

Dick: You seem to have had that line of thought concerning critics from the very beginning. You've mentioned in the past that if you cared about what critics said, you would be writing for them.

Anaya: Well, that's still true, and I think that a lot of writers, especially early in their career, have the concern and the pressure to please critics put on them. This is not healthy. We're creative people, and what comes out is who we are. Our instinct is to communicate to the world, to a bright, intelligent audience, if at all possible. In no way should we write to please a critic.

Dick: So you don't aspire to be on the front page of the *New York Times Book Review*?

Anaya: No, and again I think that comes back to those different phases of a writer's life. I am very fortunate that when I was writing *Bless Me, Ultima* I had written poetry, stories, and a couple of other novels. I was teaching when I began working on *Bless Me, Ultima* and I didn't know anything about the publishing world. So I didn't know what one did with a manuscript. I didn't know about publishers. I certainly didn't know about agents. The criticism I read was for my university classes. The critical response wasn't something that I thought would ever be applied to my work. So working from a perspective of innocence was really good for me. I was writing for myself.

Dick: You have written in a number of genres: fiction, poetry, drama, the essay. Do you consider yourself a novelist first, and does everything else flow from that?

Anaya: Probably yes. I guess I think of myself as a writer and the novel is the form which allows me to create the world that I want my characters to live in. But also I am writing children's stories now, and I enjoy those. I think the bottom line is to try to have that voice go out to the community, to reach people, to touch people with the creative act, with that creativity that becomes the book, the butterfly that touches other people's lives.

Dick: Is the fiction that you write today revised as extensively as when you wrote earlier in your career?

Anaya: Probably not. I revise a lot and I continue revising even after an editor has my manuscript. I am constantly revising in my mind, thinking of changes. I think that one gets better at what one does over the course of a lifetime, be it a carpenter or a plumber. And I guess writers should also get better. So one doesn't have to revise as intensively as when one started out young and fresh.

Dick: Do you rewrite rigorously when you create in other genres? For example, when you write poetry.

Anaya: Oh yes, if I write a poem I'll keep rewording and reworking it. Computers help because you can cut down on the work.

Sirias: I'd like to shift the focus once again. You helped define the Chicano literary voice and today that field has changed substantially. It has become crowded. As a teacher I always feel that I need to separate the Chicano from the Latino. Do you still feel a need to distinguish between groups like Cuban-Americans, Puerto Rican-Americans, and Chicanos?

Anaya: I think there may be a civil rights and political agenda in using one term like Latino to describe the Spanish-speaking people of this country, and I think that's very useful. I think that in the arts, however, there is enough of a distinct cultural background in each of those communities for that art to be viewed as coming from within that community, as having its *raíces* in that community. That includes the whole spectrum of what we call culture: the history, the language, the folklore, the mythology, the geography, and the ancestry. All of those are very distinct to the *puertorriqueño,* the *cubano,* and the *mexicano.* So I think we'll continue to see the art coming from those communities as distinct. There are a few new writers that appear as if they could be from any one of these communities. That is, the nature of their work may not be based in what we call the mythos, the totality, the essence of one people. Recently I have observed that feature in some of the poetry and a few of the novels. They read as if they are Latino, rather than having the flavor, the *sabor,* of a distinct community.

Dick: Do you mind being labeled a Chicano writer?

Anaya: No, it doesn't bother me. I think writers have always come along with the label of the particular school, or the movement, or the community they came from. In this country we have the Southern writers, we have the Harlem writers, and other such historical schools. I think that those of us who came out of the Chicano movement feel very committed to that kind of con-sciousness and to the label. So I don't have any problem with it. I think it's historically accurate. We talk about New York writers and Texan writers, so what's the difference?

Dick: Do you see that the publishing world has changed in the last ten years for the better? Is it much easier for Latino writers to get published?

Anaya: I think there's been a change. The mainstream trade publishers are recognizing Latino writers in this country. There are a lot more titles written by Latinos coming out with major trade publishers now than there were five or ten years ago. But at the same time it's still not easy to get published. I meet a lot of writers and people send me their manuscripts. The publishing world is not an easy one to enter. I worked with small presses over twenty years before I was picked up by a New York trade publisher, Warner Books. So it has been a difficult row to hoe.

Sirias: Speaking of your relationship with Warner Books, your six-book contract with them has been fulfilled with the publication of *Rio Grande Fall.* Has your relationship with them been extended? Are you going to continue publishing with Warner Books?

Anaya: Yes. But I publish with other publishers also. It all depends on what I'm doing. For example, my two children's books are published by Hyperion, and I have a couple more in the works. I just finished a children's book for Avon. I have a new manuscript out that could go either way, or to a different publisher. I think part of it is, what's the story about and where does it fit. Latino writers have also moved into the area of being represented by agents who are able to gain access to different publishers. So far, however, I am doing very well with Warner Books.

Sirias: Your spirituality is something that you have discussed amply over the course of twenty-five years of interviews. Is *Jalamanta* your attempt to convey your eclectic spiritual vision to your readers?
Anaya: Yes.

Sirias: What response has *Jalamanta* received?
Anaya: Most of what I have heard has been personal, from the people who have read it and say they like it. But it just hasn't been as widely reviewed as some of my other novels.

Sirias: I felt that it took a lot of courage to write that book, exposing your soul to everyone. Personally, I loved it. It affected me profoundly. Did you feel you were taking a big risk in writing it?
Anaya: Thank you for that personal response. That's what I get from most people. But, again, it's mostly personal. It hasn't been too widely discussed in terms of people talking about what is in there or what is not in there. I'm not sure that it took courage to write. I think if you look at all my novels, most of the philosophy of *Jalamanta* has been expressed in them in one way or another. *Jalamanta* was a way of putting it together perhaps in a more concrete form, applied to the themes in the book. I started out thinking, "I am writing about the spirit of people, their soul, their essence. What do I really mean and where does it come from and where does it go? If I don't use the answers that other philosophies or religions might give me, how do I take from those world religions and world philosophies and compose my own answer to suit me?" I think that in life this search for answers is really the journey that we're all engaged in. We're all answering those kind of very basic questions. When we get an answer it shakes us to the bottom of our souls because it is what we have to confront. One way of answering those questions is to adhere to dogma. What I've been doing in my novels and in the journeys that my characters take is to try to find the answers to those

questions. In *Jalamanta* I think I just put the questions and answers all together.

Dick: You have lived in New Mexico now for almost sixty years. Do you ever feel like uprooting yourself and moving elsewhere?
Anaya: Absolutely not.

Sirias: What is it that New Mexico provides for you? Most Americans are on the move. We have lived in five, six states by the time we're forty. What do you find in your geographical area that doesn't allow you to behave like many of us?
Anaya: For me New Mexico is home, stability, and history. It has the feel of my ancestors. Their spirits are here. They speak to me. The earth speaks to me. If all of this is happening and I live in a spiritual place, why would I leave? I recognize the necessities of life. Americans are now forced to move because you have to feed yourself and your family. I was just lucky that I was able to teach here and continue to live here. So I thank the gods for that.

Dick: Do you still teach classes at New Mexico?
Anaya: No, I retired from the university three years ago, in 1993.

Dick: I know that a question you've always been evasive about is when interviewers ask you about specific writers who have served as models for you. As new Latino and Latina writers evolve and are being consistently published, do you read any of them for inspiration?
Anaya: The problem with commenting on the writers that one likes and admires is that you often leave out somebody and then they get their feelings hurt. I think the answer remains the same as when I was a student. Now, as back then, I am reading everything, and it's not just the Chicano writers that I am reading. I wrote a poem recently, "Isis and Osiris." It's a long narrative poem, fifteen pages. For months I read the Isis and Osiris story, as well as Egyptian mythology. I think people sometimes forget that just because we are labeled Chicano writers, we know only our culture and we only read each other. I think it has to be pointed out that we love art and literature, wherever it comes from. One of the most influential novels I've read this year was written by a woman from Oklahoma. She's not Chicana, she's not Latina. It's still important for me to continue to read in all sorts of areas, and I'm probably reading more and more nonfiction. I think one of the things that is lacking in fiction in general is that somehow we are not exploring human nature the way we have to, or the way we should, or the way that is important

for our time. I wrote an essay recently in which I talk about what good is literature at the end of time if we are facing destruction, according to prophecies. We are approaching a new millenium, a change in time. Does that also entail a change in awareness and consciousness? Also, how do we live through this tremendous transition? Well, we have always survived major transitions in our history as human beings by turning to religion, by turning to art, by turning to literature, by turning to philosophy, and I guess I want to see these concerns reflected by writers, especially those who are writing fiction. When I don't see these concerns explored, I turn to nonfiction because I am like everybody else, I'm still looking for answers. I still want to grow as a person. I want to understand these elementary questions we ask ourselves about life and death. The older I get perhaps the more poignant those questions become. I want a sense of being able to face the answers with a certain serenity, with a certain peacefulness. So I like those writers who address those concerns. If they don't, I don't read them.

Dick: Tell us a little more about the Isis-Osiris poem that you wrote.

Anaya: The "Isis-Osiris" poem that I have written takes the two, Isis and Osiris, and brings them to New Mexico where they embark on a journey. It gets back again to what I have said about the Río Grande being the Nile. Osiris becomes a Kachina in the pantheon of the Pueblos. Isis becomes La Llorona along the Río Grande. It's that idea that world mythology belongs to every person. Anyone can take it and learn from those stories. You learn about the basic elements of human nature and what we've been involved with in terms of living on this earth. So we can feel that those stories aren't old, they still speak to us. We can recreate them and use them not only for our literature, but more importantly just to answer those concerns that we have as humans.

Sirias: Are you optimistic about the future of Chicano and Latino literature, particularly of its acceptance within the larger picture of American literature? Have Latinos finally carved out the literary space where their voices will be heard?

Anaya: Well, we've made a dent, and that's good. More importantly we've made a significant impact in the educational sphere. Teachers at all grade levels, not just university classes, are beginning to read Chicano, Latino literature. From that point they will perhaps teach a novel or two, maybe copy a poem and pass it out to their class. As I mentioned earlier, the mainstream trade publishers are publishing quite a few of our books. A lot of other titles are coming out both from Arte Público Press and Bilingual Review Press, who specialize in Latino literature. Other presses are becoming involved as well. I think that we've carved out an important space for ourselves. My generation of writers did something positive in putting the literature out there for the community to be aware of and to know that that's a resource they can go to. And Latinos are not only impacting literature. We are influencing art, theater, music. I think our importance is beginning to get out there in terms of the mainstream culture. That phenomenon of being invisible still exists, however. We won't be able to say until perhaps another twenty years whether or not mainstream America looks at Latinos and recognizes them, values them, and respects them. We need not be seen only as stereotypes, only as the other. So we still have a way to go.

Index